❝ As a wife and mother, I was particularly pleased to read the sections of this book HOW TO TRAVEL THE WORLD AND STAY HEALTHY dealing with Traveling with Children, Advice to the Ladies and the Handicapped Traveler. As one who has traveled all over the world with my husband, I believe this book will help prevent illness and discomfort abroad. ❞

—Mrs. Hubert H. Humphrey

❝ . . . This book is useful not only for the physician but also for the many individuals on overseas travel. As a professional in the field of Public Health and Professor of the School of Medicine of Paraguay, I do believe that HOW TO TRAVEL THE WORLD AND STAY HEALTHY is of extraordinary practical value. I think that its advice on immunization is very complete and accurate. I congratulate the authors for this work of outstanding interest. ❞

—Roque J. Avila, M.D., M.P.H.
Ambassador of Paraguay

❝ HOW TO TRAVEL THE WORLD AND STAY HEALTHY should be a valuable addition to the travel guides one takes abroad. Anyone who enjoys travel knows the good sense of avoiding illness and preserving those delightful overseas days. This distinctly is a 'good sense' book. ❞

—Mrs. Winthrop Rockefeller

How to TRAVEL the World and Stay HEALTHY

How to TRAVEL the World and Stay HEALTHY

Patrick J. Doyle, M.D., M.P.H.
and
James E. Banta, M.D., M.P.H.

AN ARC BOOK

ARCO PUBLISHING COMPANY, INC.
219 Park Avenue South, New York, N.Y. 10003

An ARC Book

Published 1974 by Arco Publishing Company, Inc.
219 Park Avenue South, New York, N.Y. 10003
by arrangement with Acropolis Books

Library of Congress Catalog Card Number 73-81464
ISBN 0-668-03342-8

Printed in the United States of America

❦❦ *The things to be seen and observed are: the courts of princes, especially when they give audience to ambassadors; the courts of justice, while they sit and hear causes, and so of consistories ecclesiastic; the churches and monasteries, with the monuments which are therein extant; the walls and fortifications of cities and towns, and so the havens and harbors; antiquities and ruins; libraries; colleges, disputations, and lectures, where any are; shipping and navies; houses and gardens of state and pleasure, near great cities; armories; arsenals; exchanges; warehouses; exercises of horsemanship, fencing, training of soldiers, and the like; comedies, such whereunto the better sort of persons do resort; treasuries of jewels and robes; cabinets and rarities; and, to conclude, whatsoever is memorable in the places where they go.*

". . . When a traveler returns home, let him not leave the countries where he has traveled altogether behind him, but maintain a correspondence by letters with those of his acquaintance which are of most worth. And let his travel appear rather in his discourse than in his apparel or gesture; and in his discourse, let him be rather circumspect in his answers than forwards to tell stories; and let it appear that he does not change his country manners for those of foreign parts, but only plant some flowers of what he has learned abroad into the customs of his own country. ❦❦

—Francis Bacon, *Of Travel* (1625)

introduction

Thousands of Americans are discovering each year the many advantages of travel outside the limits of their own country. Besides the cultural advantages of visiting or living in other countries, there are often rewarding opportunities for education and personal enrichment, recreation, and shopping which are not available at home.

Many travelers, it must be admitted, add an unnecessary burden to travel or foreign residence by being overly concerned with the alleged health hazards of foreign travel. Countless myths have been perpetuated about such dangers as the possibility of contracting exotic diseases. Equally prevalent is the more pedestrian over-anxiety about getting diarrhea in a foreign country. On the other hand, far too many travelers give no thought whatever to ordinary precautions and therefore expose themselves, at the very least, to the possibility of inconvenience and discomfort.

The purpose of this book is to serve as a guide to good general health habits for the prospective traveler or resident abroad. Preparation for travel starts, we emphasize, with visits to one's family physician, followed by securing the appropriate immunization, and then packing the traveler's personal medical kit. The wise traveler ends, as he begins, with a thorough checkup by his family physician.

While the traveler is abroad there can be problems of food selection and of general living conditions, often of extremes of climate or altitude. We consider these and other circumstances at some length. We also offer suggestions—based on personal travel experiences and also on extensive information acquired by the Georgetown University International Health Services Clinic—on what to do and what to avoid.

Throughout, it is our intention to present, in a common sense way, the average necessary precautions. If these precautions are taken, one should have a healthy and happy vacation or extended period abroad for business or pleasure.

Patrick J. Doyle, M.D., M.P.H.
James E. Banta, M.D., M.P.H.

Georgetown University, Washington, D.C.

contents

acknowledgments

The authors are indebted to the following people:

Dr. Riley Hughes, University Editor, Georgetown University, for editorial assistance.

Dee Rodenburg, of Georgetown University, for writing the chapter, Advice to the Ladies.

Frances Falt and Jeanne Rodenburg for their assistance in typing the manuscript.

going THERE

"The world is a country
which nobody ever yet knew
by description; one must travel through it one's
self to be acquainted with it."

—Lord Chesterfield

1 questions frequently asked before going abroad

"Questions are never indiscreet.
Answers sometimes are."

—Oscar Wilde

Question: In crossing time zones, what are the problems of the human biological clock? I've heard there is a new disease of travelers called circadian dysynchronization, what is it?

Answer: Scientists have been aware for some time that all living things have a biological clock. This clock regulates the normal cycle of sleeping, waking, eating, and in some species growth and development. Because of today's travel by high speed jet aircraft, it is not at all uncommon to upset one's biological clock and the normal daily variation in body functions. This is most apparent to the traveler in the disturbance of his sleep cycle.

Question: What are the symptoms of circadian dysyncronization?

Answer: Headaches, fatiguability, irritability, sleepiness and loss of appetite are common manifestations of this disturbance. Your faculties for clear thinking and decision-making may be disturbed. After being in a new time zone for a number of days the internal clock gradually readjusts and a new daily biological cycle is established.

Question: How can I prevent it?

Answer: This problem is clearly of great importance to the international traveler. The practical, indeed, the only satisfactory solution is to allow enough time for recuperation when passing through a number of time zones. Three time zone changes is about all you can manage without some upset. On any transoceanic flight you must allow a day's rest and recuperation before beginning a lot of activities and sight-seeing. Certainly if you intend to conduct any business negotiations you are not going to be at your best without having readjusted your biological clock.

It is best on a long trip to break it into several portions. You will enjoy the trip more and your health will be protected—so bon voyage.

Question: If I had a physical exam two years ago and am now on my way to a three-month vacation in South America, do I need a physical prior to departure?

Answer: Absolutely, yes.

Question: I had my shots in the Korean Army days. Isn't that enough?

Answer: No. Not medically or legally for smallpox and others. You need a booster periodically to keep your body defenses high.

Question: I'm not going to be running around stepping on rusty nails in Europe. Why do I need a tetanus shot?

Answer: You can get tetanus from other things—like a thorn in the finger!

Question: I had a slight case of polio as a child, why do I need vaccine now?

Answer: There is more than one strain. Your immunity is only for one strain.

Question: I hear many people take chances on such things as yellow fever.

Answer: Some do. You are flirting with the law but more importantly playing a dangerous game of Russian Roulette with disease.

Question: I have heard I can get everything I need in the way of medicine and medical supplies overseas. Why do I have to take any?

Answer: This is only partially true. You will save time and usually money if you take certain items with you.

Question: I hear that flying over the ocean is smoother than flying over land. Is this true?

Answer: Probably not much difference. All flying today is statistically very safe. Flying over ocean corridors often gives a pilot more chance to avoid storms.

Question: I understand everyone gets diarrhea overseas. Is this true?

Answer: Not at all. The experienced traveler seldom gets diarrhea, and when he does it is usually a slight attack. Diarrhea is a vastly over-rated ailment as is motion sickness.

Question: Can I fly with a cold?

Answer: A mild cold without fever—yes. Use nose drops and antihistamines prior to and during the flight to equalize the pressure on the eardrums.

Question: I don't mind flying over land for short

periods, but I am terrified of the ocean.

Answer: No need to worry. The exhilaration and companionship will help you forget your fears. The first trip is always the most frightening. And remember, the big jets get you there in a few hours. There is much diversion on board.

Question: I would like to fly one way and take a boat the other. What do you think?

Answer: Excellent. It's a pity more people can't take the time to enjoy the ocean cruise. It is very relaxing to return by boat.

Question: Can I drink and take motion sickness pills?

Answer: If you do it moderately. Usually two drinks or less should pose no problem if you are taking motion sickness pills.

Question: Should I plan a rest after I land in Bangkok?

Answer: Yes, definitely. Take it easy the first day because of your upset Circadian Rhythm. Take along some sleeping capsules to help you get your sleep and rest.

IT IS VERY IMPORTANT for overseas travelers to check in with their personal physician at least three months before the intended time of travel. It is absolutely essential to allow time to complete all required immunization schedules. At this initial appointment, the prospective traveler should discuss any current health problems and question the physician regarding his knowledge of specific health hazards in the countries which will be visited. The personal doctor should have adequate time to complete the immunizations or have it done by an authorized clinic. You should advise your physician of your planned itinerary as well as deviations as soon as possible.

Any medications to be taken on the trip should be stocked well in advance and unmistakably labeled with the proper dosages; for example, sleeping pills. Availability of the drug in the country to be visited should also be ascertained in advance. It is usually advisable to carry along sufficient quantities of medication for the entire trip, as a particular medicine may not be readily available locally. It is important to make sure that regular medications to be taken (antihistamines, for example) are available either in full supply for the trip or to be aware of where they can be purchased abroad. A prescription with the physician's signature would be helpful to have in case of need. If your physician also wishes to give you other medicines for possible difficulties (bismuth and paregoric for diarrhea) make sure you have enough and that you have proper instructions.

It is sometimes very valuable to have your private physician give you certain letters or certificates in addition to the immunization certificate. For example, a letter to Whom It May Concern might read as follows: "I have examined Mr. John Brown this date and have found him to be free of communicable diseases, including tuberculosis and other infections. He is in good physical and mental health." Some physicians will also have available a "Life Medical Record." This easily fits into the wallet and contains up to four pages on microfilm. In some instances, it might be valuable to have X-ray reports and even at times, electrocardiographic tracings, if these are needed. Copies of prescriptions should also be kept readily available.

Some travelers might wish their physicians to fill out for them a so-called Medical Passport. This includes medical history, physical examination, and pertinent laboratory reports. It comes in a case in which your regular passport will fit and along with other documents. This can be procured from Medical Passport Foundation, 35 East 69th Street, New York, New York 10021. The Medical Passports cost $3.50.

Another agency called MEDIFILE stores medical information on microfilm and will send necessary medical information anywhere in the world within 24 hours. The address is MEDIFILE, 120 Boylston Street, Boston, Massachusetts 02116. It is useful to have this type of information as a base-line. It often avoids the need of repeating tests or physical diagnosis. It clarifies professionally the dosage of drugs. If the traveler were to develop a bronchitis or a pneumonia abroad, a "before" type of X-ray report might obviate needless anxiety and guessing as to what was there before the trip.

Clothing

Select a wardrobe that is comfortable and easy to launder. Fortunately, today's traveler has an excellent selection of cotton and synthetic drip-dry fabrics to select from. Don't overload your suitcase with a lot of clothing, a few basic suits or dresses are adequate. Take an extra pair of shoes. We mentioned elsewhere in the book some special clothing problems. See pages: 41, 62, 77, 83, 86 and 101.

Don't forget to take along a raincoat, even if you are going to a "sunny" climate!

2

immunizations for adults

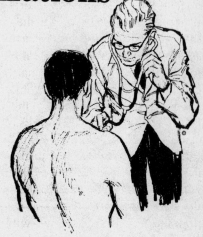

"We cannot command nature
except by obeying her."

—Francis Bacon

Smallpox

SMALLPOX IS AN ACUTE communicable viral disease.
Dr. Edward Jenner, in 1798, proved that the innoc-
ulation of human beings with materials from cow-
pox led to immunity to smallpox. Today, it is recommended that children or infants be vaccinated just
before their first birthday. With the shrinking world
becoming smaller, and with transmission of disease
easier, it is essential that everyone be vaccinated for
smallpox before departure for an overseas trip. After
vaccination, the physician or nurse will give instructions regarding the care of the vaccination. The
person vaccinated should report back to the physician

18

in about a week so that the kind of "take" may be recorded by the physician. A "take" is a reaction (swelling and redness indicates the body is reacting). There is space provided for this information on the International Immunization Certificate.

Travelers returning to the United States must show a valid International Certificate of Vaccination showing proper vaccination at least three years prior to the time of entry. Ordinarily the Certificate is checked by United States Public Health Service Officers at ports of entry to the United States. This Public Health Service Commissioned Officer is especially trained in Public Health. It is his professional, legal duty to carry out the proper form of vaccination if the traveler cannot show valid proof of vaccination within a three-year period. (Please see Appendix for the copy of the International Certificate of Vaccination). Experienced travelers will usually avail themselves of the opportunity to be vaccinated every one or two years. Vaccination should be accomplished within a month or so before departure.

In the discussion to follow we will talk about the other immunizations. There are two general concepts to consider. If a person has never received vaccine for a specific disease, an initial series, usually of two or three shots must be given in order to develop the antibodies against the disease. Usually these shots in the initial series are given at four-week intervals. This is why it is so important to begin your immunizations early so adequate spacing will be possible.

Obviously one cannot get a booster shot unless he has had the initial series. A booster or recall shot for a specific disease raises the antibody level. Below we will tell you the time sequences and duration of effect of the boosters.

Tetanus-Diphtheria

Although smallpox cases seldom occur in the United States, this is not the case with tetanus and diphtheria.

If there is any doubt about the immunity, a booster diphtheria and tetanus shot should be given. Usually this is combined for adults in a diphtheria-tetanus toxoid injection. Tetanus toxoid is a very effective immunizing substance. A single series of injections for both diphtheria and tetanus is now recommended. This is a combination of tetanus and diphtheria given in one shot and repeated after one month and one year. Occasionally there will be redness, swelling, pain, and heat at the site of injection. This is considered a normal reaction. It can be treated by applying cold compresses locally at the site of swelling and by taking one or two aspirins every four hours or so as required. Tetanus boosters are required every ten years and after a penetrating wound.

Typhoid

Typhoid fever continues to be an important disease in many parts of the world where sanitation is inadequate and water supplies are poorly engineered and unchlorinated. Even in Western Europe and the United States there are occasional acute outbreaks of typhoid affecting many people. Unfortunately, typhoid vaccine is not as effective as some vaccines, and immunizations therefore have to be repeated at more frequent intervals. The initial series consists of a total of two shots each given four weeks apart. For individuals requiring a booster, 1/10 cc of vaccine is injected into the skin, producing a small bleb. Sometimes some people will have a moderate reaction to typhoid vaccine, with fever and a feeling of malaise.

Typhoid vaccine is no longer recommended for Europe, nor for other areas if the traveler stays at usual tourist accommodations. This should be discussed with your family physician.

Polio

In the United States, poliomyelitis has been eliminated as a serious threat to health because of the effectiveness of present vaccines. Immunization is not universally practiced, and polio is still present in many countries. It is strongly recommended that all travelers be completely protected against poliomyelitis before traveling. There are two kinds of vaccines: The Salk Vaccine, a killed virus vaccine given by injection; and the Sabin Vaccine, a live virus vaccine given orally. In general, the Sabin Vaccine is more widely used, but all people should be immunized with either the Salk or Sabin Vaccine. If oral vaccine (Sabin) has been completed, one booster dose is recommended for international travel. We shall discuss the polio vaccine later when we discuss immunization in children.

Infectious Hepatitis

The occurrence of infectious hepatitis varies across the world. However, there are many physicians who feel that the occurrence of hepatitis is greater in Asia, Africa and South America than it is in North America. Your physician may wish to give you gamma globulin, which offers some protection. Gamma globulin is obtained from the pooled plasma portion of blood and is the fraction of blood containing antibodies. Antibodies provide protection from infectious disease, and when gamma globulin is used other people's antibodies are being borrowed, so to speak. Usually

5 to 10 cc injection into the muscle will be necessary prior to departure. This should be repeated every four to six months while overseas.

Influenza

There is much difference of opinion concerning the routine use of influenza vaccine. This is complicated by the fact that the type of influenza present is likely to change from year to year. In general, it is recommended that the vaccine be given to people with debilitating disease, chronic lung disease, and the like. Your physician probably will not wish to use this vaccine, unless you have such a health problem.

Non-routine Immunizations

There will be times when other immunizations are needed. Among some of these might be typhus, cholera, plague, yellow fever, and perhaps tuberculosis. These immunizations are not routinely given, but may be required and warranted when epidemics or unusually high prevalent rates exist in specific countries.

Typhus Immunization

Typhus is a hazard for travelers to Asia, Africa, the Middle East, Mexico, and the Andean Region of South America. There are actually two types of typhus: one called epidemic, and transmitted by the louse; the other called endemic and transmitted by the rat flea. Originally vaccination was recommended for persons going to areas suspected of being infected with louse-borne (epidemic) typhus. Basic immunization consists of two inoculations not less than four weeks apart. Persons staying in infected areas should have a booster inoculation every six to 12 months.

Service recommends plague vaccine only for Viet Nam, Laos and Cambodia unless the traveler will have occupational exposure to rodents in areas in which plague occurs. After an initial immunization you will require a booster dose every four to six months while in an infected area.

Yellow Fever Immunization

Yellow fever immunization was one of the first diseases to be subject to international sanitary regulations. In many countries of the Western Hemisphere and in Africa these regulations are in effect.

Those going to Central and South America, Africa, and the Pacific should be immunized. Once properly immunized against yellow fever, protection is afforded for ten years.

Yellow fever immunizations can only be given in certified centers. The reason for this relates to the care necessary in the proper refrigeration and mixing of the vaccine prior to injection. Each vial has the dry powdered vaccine. When properly diluted, the mixture is enough for five injections. After the liquid is added to the powder, the mixture of five doses must be used within one hour. Hence, the need for designated centers. These centers are designated by the U.S. Public Health Service. Your physician can tell you the nearest one.

One must be careful that Yellow Fever Vaccine is not given at the same time as Smallpox in order to avoid several possible postvaccinial reactions, such as encephalitis.

Yellow fever inoculation should precede smallpox by at least four days. If this is not possible, a period of at least 21 days must elapse between smallpox vaccination, done first, and the subsequent yellow fever inoculation.

Since February 1969 Typhus vaccine is recommended only for those whose work abroad places them in areas where the local population is infected.

Cholera

Cholera is one of the diseases subject to agreement under the International Sanitary Regulations of the World Health Organization. This means that vaccination is required by all countries after a traveler has passed through or come from an area where cholera is present, necessitating immunization for entry. The initial course is two injections, with at least a seven-day interval between the two. A booster dose must be given every six months. International regulation requires that a valid cholera vaccination certificate be issued within the past six months. Immunization must have been given at least six days before arrival at the port of entry. Some authorities are very strict about this, and an individual may be held in quarantine when a valid certificate is not shown.

Plague Immunization

Plague is a disease which occurs in many parts of the world, including the United States of America. It is usually contracted by individuals who are hunters or naturalists and have contact with small rodents. In some areas human plague also exists, and it can be transmitted by the flea or through the respiratory route. You should only be immunized if you are going to an area where plague is occurring and if you are likely to be exposed. You should only be immunized after discussing it with your personal physician and knowledgeable health authorities such as the U.S. Public Health Service. Currently, the Public Health

24

It is questionable whether a pregnant woman (especially in the first three months) should receive Yellow Fever Immunization.

Rabies

Rabies is a very serious problem in many parts of the world. This is true where there is a large uncontrolled dog population allowed to run free and unimmunized against rabies. Individuals visiting rural areas or smaller provincial towns definitely risk being bitten by these animals. Rabies, once contracted, is always fatal. By giving a series of immunizations (i.e., 14 to 21 shots), persons may be protected from acquiring rabies after having been bitten by a rabid animal. This measure usually works. It should be pointed out that there has never been a fatal case of rabies in individuals who have been immunized prior to exposure to rabies and who subsequently receive the anti-rabies series of shots after exposure.

If you are going to be spending time in rural areas or in smaller towns and villages in many parts of Latin America, Africa, and Asia, then pre-exposure immunization against rabies may be advisable. This is accomplished by three shots of duck-embryo rabies vaccine. After the initial shot is given, it is repeated at one month and a third shot seven months later. Many veterinarians, cave explorers exposed to bats, and Peace Corps volunteers follow this procedure. This does not obviate the requirement for post-exposure immunization. Pre-exposure immunization is suggested for Americans *resident* in South America, Africa and Asia.

Tuberculosis Vaccine

There is still controversy concerning the use of BCG (Bacillus Calmette-Guerin) Vaccine against tuberculosis. Tuberculosis continues to be a very important cause of disease and death in most parts of the world. A traveler intending to live for an extended period of time in a less developed country, a professional health worker who will be working in a health program, or a student who will be working in an overseas educational program might well ask, "Should I be protected against the possibility of contracting TB?"

Unfortunately the answer is complex. First, the traveler should have a TB skin test at the first visit to the physician before travel. The skin test, whereby material is injected into the skin, is preferable over the Patch Test. If one has a positive test, this is taken as evidence of naturally acquired allergy and is a sign of some immunity.

Those who will be living under conditions described above and who have a negative skin test for TB might be considered candidates for the BCG Vaccine. The family physician is the best one to make this decision. If the vaccine is to be given, it is best given two weeks after a negative TB skin test. It *should not* be given one month before or after a smallpox vaccination, in order to avoid a severe post vaccinial reaction such as encephalitis.

Many U.S. physicians feel it is best for the person with a negative skin test not to take BCG Vaccine. In the event a person who has previously had a negative reaction shows a positive one at a subsequent test or should X-ray findings be indicative of beginning infection, he or she may be placed on oral drugs, which will effectively control any problem. Once BCG Vaccine is given, however, the skin test is no longer an effective indicator, because the BCG Vaccine causes the skin test to be positive.

3 immunizations for children

"A little neglect may breed mischief."

—Benjamin Franklin

MANY CHILDREN TODAY ARE RECEIVING the so-called DPT—diphtheria, pertusis (whooping cough) and tetanus along with the polio vaccine. Ordinarily, immunization against influenza is not necessary. It would be wise to have the child receive vaccination against measles. This is best done under the supervision of the pediatrician or family physician.

Smallpox

The best age for the first vaccination is between five and six months of age. The older child and adult should be vaccinated every three to five years. Occasionally a child will not be able to tolerate Smallpox Vaccination. This is true if the child has a congenital lack of gamma globulin or severe eczema. A certificate by the family physician to this effect will usually be honored by port authorities.

DPT—Diptheria, Pertussis (Whooping Cough), Tetanus

The following schedule is recommended:

2-3 months—1st DPT plus oral Polio Vaccine
(Sabin)
3-4 months—2nd DPT
4-5 months—3rd DPT plus oral Polio Vaccine
(Sabin)

In older children and adolescents who will travel, the recommendations made earlier on Diphtheria-Tetanus shots suffice. (See Page 20)

Typhoid-Paratyphoid

Vaccine is usually not given under 4-5 months. Infants up to one year will get four injections at intervals of one to four weeks. Older children will be handled as adults. If travel is prolonged, yearly boosters are indicated.

Infectious Hepatitis

Infants seldom get this and when seen in children, it is milder than in adults. However, if appropriate for the circumstances, the physician might wish to use gamma globulin.

Influenza

Routine immunization is not necessary. Nonetheless, children with diseases such as chronic heart, kidney, or lung disease might need it. Attention should be paid to the possible allergic reactions to it.

Tuberculosis

TB-negative babies and those children who may be exposed to TB are potential candidates for the BCG Vaccine. This decision rests with the family physician.

Measles

All children should be vaccinated against measles. Dosages and schedules are changing often, since the vaccine is relatively new and undergoing continual improvement. The family physician will have decided *how* to use the vaccine.

Other Immunizations

Typhus. Three injections with intervals of one to three weeks are indicated.

Yellow Fever. Children over six months going to endemic areas should be vaccinated.

Cholera. If indicated, can be given to children over six months of age. If risk continues, boosters should be given every six months.

Plague. If indicated, children over six months of age should be inoculated with two injections seven days apart.

4 medicines to take along

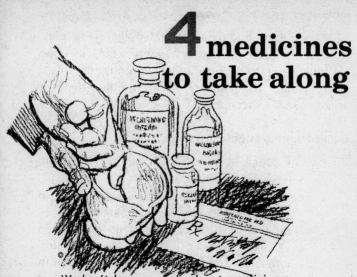

"I don't know much about medicine, but I know what I like."

—S. J. Perelman

THE TYPE AND AMOUNT OF MEDICATIONS to be taken along, of course, depend on the health status, the itinerary, and the duration of the trip. Drugs and medications may be available abroad and usually at reasonable prices. However, the names, potency, and dosage schedule may vary significantly from drugs and medications that one's personal physician usually prescribes. Therefore, it would seem advisable to take along enough medication to last the duration of the trip abroad. One's personal physician should supply detailed instructions on diagnosis and treatment, including medications and dosage schedules. The physician should prescribe giving the *generic* name of medications to be used. If one is living abroad for an extended period, it would be wise to find a physician not only in case of emergencies or illness but also for advice on possible changes or adjustments in medicines taken over a long period. An example of this would be someone taking an antihistamine for an allergy. The dosage might need to be increased if symptoms persist.

Motion Sickness

Air sickness, sea sickness, train sickness, and car sickness are all forms of motion sickness. Fortunately less than ten per cent of travelers experience sea sickness, less than two per cent air sickness, and less than one per cent train or auto. Dizziness and nausea may be greatly reduced by presently available anti-motion sickness drugs. Airliners and ocean liners have supplies of these medications. Dimenhydrinate, U.S.P. 50 mg. tablets, Meclivine HCl 25 mg. tablets, or Cyclizine 50 mg. tablets are typical anti-motion sickness drugs. They can be taken three or four times a day while flying or sailing.

Many motion sickness remedies cause drowsiness, and they should not be used while driving an automobile.

Diarrhea

Perhaps the most frequent minor illness that the traveler experiences is simple diarrhea. One should take a small amount of Kaolin-Pectin mixture, Paregoric, or Lomotil (brand of Diphenoxylate hydrochloride with atropine sulfate). The latter may also be taken in pill form. Either type can be taken usually three times a day; they are very helpful for the cramps which sometimes accompany diarrhea. They should not be used too often or too long or a maximum of two days usage. The liquids usually require no special handling except that the cover should be sealed with cellophane tape to prevent leakage. This is a good precaution for all liquid medications.

Malaria

Malaria continues to occur in many parts of the world, and it may be a threat to the traveler. This threat can be eliminated by taking prophylactic medication, which will prevent infection if taken before exposure to a malarious area.

It has been found that a combination of chloroquine phosphate and primaquine phosphate is highly effective for malaria prophylaxis.

The drug is usually administered as the following tablet:

Chloroquine phosphate, U.S.P. (300 mg. base) 500 mg.

Primaquine phosphate, (45 mg. base) 79 mg.

Recommended Dosage:

Starting at least one day before entering the malarious area, one tablet weekly, taken on the same day each week. This schedule (one tablet weekly, on the same day) should be continued for six weeks after leaving the hazardous area.

Precautions:

The drug should not be taken by people with anemia, blood disease, rheumatoid arthritis, or allergic diseases. Individuals with certain blood cell chemistry deficiency should not take the tablets. The drug should be discontinued immediately and a physician consulted if darkening of the urine or skin reaction occurs.

An occasional individual may experience intestinal cramps and one or two loose bowel movements several hours after ingestion of tablet; this should cause no alarm.

Warning:

Children are especially sensitive to this drug. It

must be kept out of reach of children, as accidental ingestion could be very dangerous.

Water Purification

Boiling is the safest way to purify water, but if water purification tablets are needed, one should use Halazone (Abbott). Boiling or using purification will insure killing of the bacteria which cause infectious diarrhea. Two or more of these tablets per quart of water usually will purify the water within a half hour. Directions which are on the package should be followed. One other good, simple water purification technique is the use of tincture of iodine, U.S.P. Use three drops of iodine per quart of water. This should stand at least thirty minutes before drinking. Use eight to ten drops for cloudy water. The water may have a slight iodine taste but it will be safe for drinking or brushing your teeth.

Toilet Tissues or Disposable Paper Tissues

Because in many places in the world disposable paper tissue and toilet tissue are unavailable, it is prudent to take along a small supply. If one is disposed to problems with hemorrhoids this is particularly true.

5 your personal medical kit

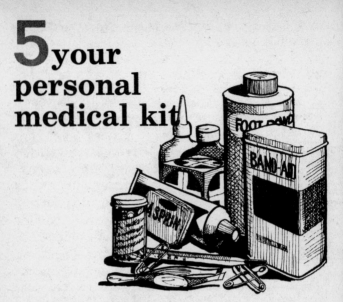

"Simplify, simplify."

—Thoreau

MOST PEOPLE EXPERIENCE a number of minor illnesses each year, and you probably do, too. Under most circumstances whether at home or abroad you can "weather through" these episodes without any special treatment or the need to consult a physician. Mother Nature has given you a remarkable capacity to overcome the insult of minor illnesses.

You may take along a "medical kit" which will serve to help through minor illnesses and perhaps save you having to contact a physician for minor episodes. If there is any question, however, do not hesitate to seek a physician's advice.

We have listed some items which might be included in a personal "medical kit" for your trip. All of the drugs and other items are available without a physician's prescription. They come in a variety of brand names, though, and thus you may require some assistance from your pharmacist in selecting appropriate items.

MEDICAL KIT

Item

1. Aspirin, 5 gr.
2. Aluminum Hydroxide with Magnesium Trisilicate tablets
3. Milk of Magnesia tablets
4. Chlorpheniramine tablets
5. Antihistamine nasal spray
6. Antimicrobial Skin Ointment
7. Calamine Lotion, 4 oz.
8. Surgical soap, liquid
9. Tweezers
10. Antifungal Skin Ointment, 2 oz.
11. Zincundecate foot powder, 2 oz.
12. Vitamin mineral tablets
13. Oil of Cloves and Benzocaine Mixture
14. Opthalmic Ointment, 1/8 oz.
15. Throat Lozenge
16. Kaolin-Pectin Mixture, tablets or liquid
17. Paregoric or Lomotil
18. Band-Aid
19. Elastic Bandage, 3" w
20. Gauze Bandage, 2" x 10 yd.
21. Gauze Pad, 4" x 4"
22. Adhesive tape
23. Safety Pins, medium, 12's
24. Thermometer
25. Insect Repellent
26. Sleeping pills (need prescription)

B. Directions for Drugs in Medical Kit

1. **Aspirin.** This is one of the most widely used and effective drugs for the relief of muscular pains and

other ill-defined aches (e.g., headache). It is also one of the better drugs used for symptomatic treatment of fever.

Directions: One or two tablets three or four times a day for control of pain. Usually one or two doses are adequate.

Precaution: Do not take large doses of aspirin nor take tablets on a frequent dosage schedule over a long period of time.

2. **Aluminum Hydroxide with Magnesium Trisilicate.** These tablets are an antacid and are used for the relief of stomach distress such as "heartburn," "acid stomach," "upset stomach," etc.

Directions: Chew one or two tablets and wash down with a glass of water three or four times a day.

Precaution: (1) Should upper abdominal or stomach distress continue for two or three days in spite of the drug and bland diet, seek medical attention. (2) Some individuals become constipated if the drug is taken for a prolonged period.

3. **Milk of Magnesia.** These tablets are an effective, mild laxative. They should not be taken if there are abdominal cramps or pain.

4. **Chlorpheniramine.** This drug is valuable for the symptomatic relief of a number of allergic conditions such as hayfever, hives, poison oak or ivy, and other types of contact dermatitis. It may also be used to help relieve the nasal congestion and irritated eyes of a common cold.

Directions: One tablet three or four times a day as necessary to relieve symptoms.

Precaution: The drug can cause drowsiness. Dosages should be adjusted to minimize this side effect. If full dosage is required for relief of symptoms with attendant drowsiness, activities requiring muscular co-ordination or mental concentration should be restricted (viz., driving).

5. **Antihistamine nasal spray.** This is useful for treatment of nasal congestion and as an aid in opening up nasal sinuses and eustacian tubes in upper respiratory infections.

Directions: Spray lightly into each nostril; may be repeated four or five times daily.

6. **Antimicrobial Skin Ointment.** This ointment should be used in treatment of superficial skin infections and burns.

Directions: (1) In the case of skin infections, wash the lesion well with surgical soap and with water that has been boiled. Dry the area with a sterile gauze pad from the Kit. Apply the ointment liberally and bandage. Re-bandage each day and apply ointment each time the wound is dressed. (2) For burns, wash the area carefully with soap and with water that has been boiled. Be careful not to break any blisters. Apply ointment liberally and bandage with several layers of gauze. Redress as bandage becomes soiled. In the event of an extensive burn, seek medical attention without delay.

7. **Calamine Lotion.** This lotion provides effective relief for mild sunburn, prickly heat, the itching associated with hives, insect bites, and mild poison oak or ivy. It may also be used for other mild skin irritations.

Directions: Clean the area well with soap and water and dry thoroughly. Apply the lotion to the affected area as needed.

8. **Surgical Soap.** This contains Hexachlorophene, an efficient antibacterial agent. Skin infections should be washed two or three times daily, using the soap. Leave the soap on for three minutes before thoroughly rinsing with cooled, *boiled* water.

9. **Tweezers.** For the removal of small particles of foreign matter imbedded in the skin. Affected area

should be cleansed thoroughly, preferably with liquid surgical soap and cooled, boiled water.

10. **Antifungal Skin Ointment.** To be used for the treatment of fungus infections of the skin. It may also be used in similar skin infections of the crotch and armpits.

Directions: Wash the affected area with soap and water, rinse well, and *dry thoroughly*. The ointment should be rubbed into the area. This should be done each night before retiring.

11. **Zincundecate Foot Powder.** This should be applied liberally to the affected area for daytime treatment. It may also be used as a prophylaxis for daytime use as a foot dusting powder.

12. **Vitamin-Mineral Tablets.** This is a supplemental tablet containing recommended vitamins and minerals which will reinforce and assure an adequate daily supply of vitamins and certain minerals essential to maintaining good nutritional balance. Dosage is one tablet per day. It is to be noted that *additional intake over the above dosage will be of no additional nutritional value. In fact, the excessive intake of vitamin tablets (or vitamin-mineral tablets) over the recommended dosage may be harmful.*

It is particularly important that the vitamin-mineral tablets be taken during those times where a balanced diet cannot be maintained.

13. **Oil of Cloves and Benzocaine Mixture.** This medication has been included in the Medical Kit as a preparation to use for the temporary relief of dental pain (resulting from caries or recent surface exposure of nerve ends of a tooth). Clean cavity and place small amount of wax in it.

14. **Opthalmic Ointment.** This medication may be used in the treatment of eye infections or where a protective ointment coating of the conjunctiva may

be desired. In ophthalmic infections, this ointment should be applied every three to four hours inside the lower eyelid for several days.

15. **Throat Lozenge.** Follow directions on package. Do not use more than maximum indicated for 24-hour period.

16. **Kaolin-Pectin Mixture.** This medication may be used for the temporary relief of diarrhea. Do not use for more than two days or in the presence of high fever. If diarrhea persists, or if there is blood and mucus, see a physician at once.

17. **Paregoric or Lomotil.** These medications may be used in conjunction with Kaolin-Pectin or alone for the relief of the cramps associated with diarrhea. They slow the motility of the bowel. They should not be used more than several days.

6
traveling
by
air

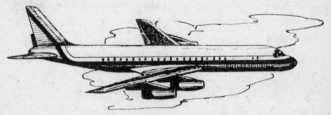

"Swift be thy flight!"

—Shelley

THERE ARE VERY FEW health or medical reasons for not flying. In this day and age, the hazards of flying are quite minimal. In February 1961, the Committee of Medical Criteria for passenger flying of the Aerospace Medical Association published a complete list of conditions under which flying would be hazardous. Obviously, any patient who should be in the hospital should not be traveling on an airplane. This would, of course, include many conditions: mental patients and those with a contagious disease, for example. Persons who have recovered from coronary heart disease can ordinarily travel, provided there are oxygen and pressurized cabins available. These are available in most parts of the world, but plans should be made in advance. Persons who have severe disturbances of heart rhythm, severe hypertension or markedly enlarged hearts should be carefully evaluated prior to air travel. Severe anemia may be a contraindication to flying. Infants seven days of age usually can be transported by air without too much difficulty. Most airlines accept pregnant women during the seventh month of pregnancy and many will transport women in the eighth month. Usually pregnancy beyond this period requires a certification by a physician.

Among some of the other considerations to remember concerning the ability to fly are the following:

- Tolerance of seats and seat belts. Will the traveler be able to accommodate to the prolonged seated positions as well as the use of seat belts? People over 35 who have varicose veins and are taking long trips by plane, car or bus should use individually fitted elastic stockings. During the trip, such a passenger should get up and walk around frequently if possible. This will help the circulation and also prevent any possible spread of emboli to the lungs. Travelers who have varicose veins will find traveling first class a benefit because there is more room to stretch and move about.
- Noise and vibration. In general these are minimal today.
- Emotional stability. A person who is undergoing severe emotional illness probably is not a good candidate for a long air trip unless absolutely necessary, and then a responsible traveling companion is essential.

In general, then, if good sense is used and proper consultation is made with a physician, most persons having an illness or chronic disability such as diabetes, epilepsy, etc., can tolerate travel and their disabilities will not be aggravated by air travel.

41

If a traveler suffers from a disease which occasionally causes loss of consciousness such as epilepsy or diabetes, he should have a card in the wallet or pocket-book identifying the illness.

"MEDIC-ALERT" Company has available stainless steel bracelets or emblems which in addition to an engraved serial number also have key words such as "Diabetic," etc. The serial number enables the attendent physician to call collect night or day for more specific information about the patient.

7
traveling by ship

"Never a ship sails out of the bay
But carries my heart as a stowaway."
—Roselle Mercer Montgomery

FOR THOSE WHO HAVE THE TIME, traveling on a modern cruise ship can be a relaxing experience. There are a few points to discuss which relate to questions most frequently asked.

Availability of Physicians

All major passenger liners have physicians as well as nurses on board. The physician can usually be identified by a cadeuses and the three gold stripes on his sleeve.

In addition to the physician and nurse there will be a well-stocked pharmacy and a sick bay. Most emergency surgical procedures can be done. There is an excellent radio hook-up to summon Coast Guard help if transportation is needed.

Many ship companies require certificates from your family physician. This applies to persons over

65 years of age, small infants, and those with special problems. Detailed instructions should be available to the ship's physician for special medical problems, diet, or unusual types of therapy. Most ships will not allow a woman beyond her seventh month of pregnancy.

Ships' physicians are allowed to charge standard fees for attention to those conditions which existed prior to embarkation. There is usually no fee for any care given for new illness aboard ship.

Most freighters will not have a physician on board, but they will have pharmacist mates who are well trained to do their job. They usually require a medical certificate for people of advanced years. Inquire directly or through your travel agent if contemplating this mode of travel.

The Handicapped

Most ships have wheelchairs on board. The numerous call buttons, guard rails, and bathroom handles placed for the normal traveler are bonuses for the handicapped. Some companies allow reduced rates for attendants accompanying the handicapped. This is especially true for the blind.

The traveler by water also is protected. There are many advantages for the handicapped person in equipment and special attention on board ship. Another advantage is that most cruise ships often have a physician on board and a sick bay.

Drinking Water and Sanitation

Ships come under the jurisdiction of port authorities, and the laws on health and sanitation are strict. Tap water is safe to use. For those who prefer it, bottled mineral water is available. Dining rooms, kitchens, food storage rooms come under constant and strict surveillance for sanitation.

Eating

There are many temptations to overindulge in food. The sea air increases appetites. Those who are weight watchers should use moderation. Special dietary items for health or religious reasons can be arranged beforehand. Liquor is inexpensive, and again, one should use moderation.

Motion Sickness

There is a large psychological component here. It is interesting to note that often westbound travelers, immigrants especially, will often have motion sickness, owing to anxiety and stress.

One should avoid large amounts of liquids. Moderate amounts of alcoholic beverages are usually well tolerated and often have a relaxing effect.

Fresh air is also helpful. Motion sickness pills are available. With the new type of stabilizers on most ships, motion sickness is less and less of a problem on cruises.

PLAY IT SAFE!
KNOW YOUR SIGNS!

FIRST AID STATION

One of the great killers in the world today is accidents and traffic accidents are the major cause, at home and abroad. Motoring abroad can be an interesting and pleasant experience but driving will be different. Caution and extra care are a must if you want a safe trip. Know the local traffic laws and rules of the road. Even if you are a pedestrian and go for a walk know the traffic signs. They are different than what you are probably familiar with. Follow the signs.

INTERNATIONAL SIGNS OF THE ROAD

Although the coloring is not entirely uniform, the signs themselves are easily recognized by their shapes and symbols:

△ Triangular—for danger signs

○ Circular—for signs giving definite instructions

□ Rectangular—for informative signs

Some more common examples:

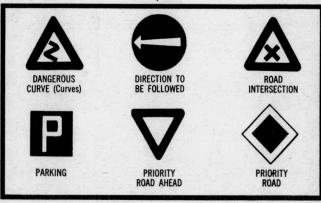

DANGEROUS CURVE (Curves)

DIRECTION TO BE FOLLOWED

ROAD INTERSECTION

PARKING

PRIORITY ROAD AHEAD

PRIORITY ROAD

over THERE

"Though we travel
the world over to find the beautiful
we must carry it with us
or we find it not."

—Emerson

8
questions frequently asked when abroad

Question: My sister has a friend with a relative in Bolivia who is a doctor. Should I use him on my forthcoming trip?
Answer: That's taking a chance. Better go through the Embassy or Intermedic, Inc.

Question: Someone. said if I stick with bottled beer overseas, I'd be O.K. Is this true?
Answer: Yes, but you may not draw a sober breath. Seriously, you can use bottled water just as well.

Question: Can I brush my teeth with tap water in India?
Answer: No. Use bottled water for this or put iodine in the tap water first.

Question: Should I bring along antibiotics in case I catch a cold on my trip?

Answer: Antibiotics won't help a common cold. If you need antibiotics, a physician should prescribe them. They are easy to get overseas.

Question: Should I bring my own Scotch for medicinal purposes?
Answer: Check the regulations for the country. Scotch is difficult to get and very expensive in most parts of the world.

Question: It seems inevitable that I shall get diarrhea on my trip overseas. Wouldn't it be better to take something prophylactically?
Answer: We do not recommend this. Prevention is the rule. Stick to the rules laid down in the chapter.

Question: What about venereal disease in other parts of the world?
Answer: In most parts of the world, the rates are high. Extreme caution and restraint must be used, even with "nice" people. Prostitution is prevalent.

Question: Should I have a dental check-up before departure?
Answer: This is essential. Have all cavities filled and have the teeth cleaned. It could save you a toothache.

Question: Is my group hospitalization valid abroad?
Answer: In some places. You should check ahead of time with the issuing agency of your hospitalization plan; you may be able to obtain forms for use abroad.

Question: Can I collect abroad on my Medicare in case of a long hospital stay overseas?
Answer: Check with your local agency of the Social Security Administration on this one.

Question: What about drinking fruit juices abroad? Should I risk it?

Answer: No. Don't drink anything you can't peel yourself.

Question: Should I take extra sunglasses?

Answer: Good idea. If you use prescription lenses, take along a copy of the prescription.

Question: What is the best way to avoid sunburn?

Answer: Short daily exposures. Frequent use of protective cream is preferable. Protect eyes with good sunglasses or moist eye pads.

Question: What about thermal underwear for extremely cold climate?

Answer: This is good to take along; it may be difficult to get overseas.

Question: I have mild hypertension. Would a month in Mexico City hurt me?

Answer: You should have little or no difficulty. Take it easy in this altitude the first week. This includes the use of alcohol.

Question: Should I take heating pads or electric sheets or blanket?

Answer: These may prove to be a headache at most overseas hotels because their electrical systems vary considerably from ours. The same applies to heat lamps. If necessary, check on different voltages and plugs.

Question: Can I take a wheelchair overseas?

Answer: Yes. This is no problem. Check with your travel agent, airline or ship.

Question: My husband has mild angina and is on medication. Can we fly to Paris?

Answer: Your husband should have no discomfort. Very many people fly with heart disease.

Question: I am a diabetic. My insulin dosage is still not yet well regulated. Should I take an extended trip to Pakistan?

Answer: It would be wiser to wait until your physician has your insulin dosage regulated and stabilized.

Question: I have asthma. At times I have to take adrenaline injections. Could I travel to Israel for a vacation?

Answer: This should pose no difficulty. Your physician may wish to instruct you in the use of an inhaler in lieu of a shot. When you get to Israel, you will find excellent physicians.

Question: My father is 88 and wants to take an ocean cruise through the Mediterrean this spring. What do you think?

Answer: If his physician says yes, by all means take him. We'd like to join you.

Question: My child has epilepsy, with mild seizures about once a month. My husband has been given a sabbatical to teach in Lebanon for a year. Please advise.

Answer: People with seizures tolerate travel very well. You should have no difficulties. Have your family physician prepare a summary of the child's condition and medications. Contact the American University in Beirut for a physician to handle the child during your year there.

Question: I have a Mongoloid child who is now six years old. We are planning a month in Spain. Please advise.

Answer: These children are usually very easy to handle and tolerate travel very well. There are no special instructions on this.

Question: My five-year-old has one cold after another. My husband wants to take us to Germany for two months. What do you think?

Answer: Frequent colds may be due to allergy. Germany is cold in the winter. You should have no more difficulty there in the warm weather than here.

Question: My husband is a great sports enthusiast but only goes at it when the mood is on him. He is 61 years young. We plan to spend three months in Switzerland and France. How do I slow him down?

Answer: We presume you mean he goes at the vigorous sports in a sporadic fashion. We suggest you show him a few obituaries of his friends from the last two years.

Diet

AS ONE READS THE TRAVEL ADS, especially for ocean trips, he is struck by the great amounts and varieties of food available on board tour ships. Certainly one is going to enjoy himself. However, moderation should be used in eating. The same principle applies to drinking. If one is using medication for *motion sickness*, alcohol must be used sparingly. If one is accustomed to drinking cocktails before dinner, this custom could be continued whether traveling by plane or ship. Most overseas airline flights will allow you to have two drinks before dinner. Very often these drinks will help calm a person who might have some trepidation about flying over the ocean. Again, one must be very cautious when using these with sedatives or motion sickness pills. Excessive drinking prior to flying is hazardous. Bringing one's own supply of alcohol on board the airliner is not only illegal, it can be dangerous. Any traveler with a tendency toward stomach or gall bladder trouble must be careful about the types of food eaten. To minimize the possibility of motion sickness, the traveler should avoid heavy, fried, or greasy foods as well as large quantities of liquids.

Motion Sickness

Very few have difficulty with motion sickness. There are many excellent drugs available, among them several widely used anti-motion sickness medications. Before and during the air trip, one should eat and drink moderately. Conversation with an interesting companion often will help take one's mind off the possibility of becoming motion sick. Aboard ship, choosing a cabin or state room inboard, not far from the waterline is sometimes helpful. Fresh air, often, will help a traveler who has been a little seasick. Again, motion sickness is rare and usually very mild, except in very heavy weather.

In addition to drugs, dietary self-discipline is a key to continued success in dealing with motion sickness. On recovery, the traveler should continue to observe careful dietary restrictions. Toast, boiled potatoes, tapioca, lean chicken, and lamb chops may be well tolerated.

Air Otitis

Some travelers will experience difficulties in descent in an airplane even when the plane is pressurized. Owing to the unequal pressure on the eardrum a feeling of fullness sometimes develops, and occasionally, transient pain. Individuals who have experienced ear infections or ear problems associated with pressure changes should have an examination by their personal physician before undertaking an extensive air trip abroad.

For most people, chewing gum, yawning, and frequent swallowing will often help minimize any changes in the pressure. If pain persists or hearing is affected after the flight (say, for several hours), it might be necessary to have the attention of a physician. Again, this is extremely rare.

Travelers who have a sinus condition will sometimes feel uncomfortable in flight, especially if pressure is not well equalized. The use of nose drops or an inhaler to shrink nasal mucosa just before the flight will often minimize the discomfort of otitis or sinusitis. Antihistamines are also helpful, but do not combine them with motion sickness pills.

Disturbed Cycle

The physiologists speak of a so-called Circadian Rhythm which in humans and animals involves many biophysiological activities, including sleep, alertness, body temperature, and release of stress hormones. Swift air travel between time zones often tends to upset this cycle. Thus, a traveler rushing to India through many time zones may experience fatigue, depression, headache, and the like. This is temporary, but it should be taken into account and compensated for by sensible schedule adjustments and proper rest on arrival. It may be necessary to take a sleeping pill to induce sleep. It is important to insure a good night's rest to readjust one's cycle.

Again, the advertisements say half the fun is getting there. In general, they are true. The companionship on board plane and ship with the excellent service aboard, in most cases, will ensure a comfortable trip.

9 living or traveling abroad

"The traveler sees what he sees; the tripper sees what he has come to see."

—G. K. Chesterton

HERE WE SHALL DEAL WITH A VARIETY of items, including how to find a physician overseas, living conditions, common illnesses one may encounter abroad, and finally a general word on hygiene. There is great variation between regions of the world, so it is difficult to be dogmatic. Europe is very much like North America. However, the countries of the remaining areas of Asia, Africa, and North, Central, and South America vary greatly.

Finding a Physician Overseas

Finding a physician overseas is best first discussed with the family physician. Often he or she will know of a colleague in an overseas area, or will check with the local medical school which often has contacts in overseas centers. The embassy offices in Washington also are helpful prior to the trip. The *American Hospital Association* keeps a list of hospitals which are approved overseas. In addition, one may contact *Intermedic* of New York City. *Intermedic* has formed an international network of physicians who ensure the participating traveler accurate diagnosis and conscientious treatment whenever needed. All the physicians certified speak English. These physicians also agree to work for the following fees:

Office Visit.. $ 8.00

House or Hotel Visit

    Daytime.. $10.00

    Nighttime $15.00

It is important to note that these physicians respond to emergencies and all have good hospital connections. Personal membership in *Intermedic* for one year costs $5.00 or $9.00 for a family membership. Members are given a Directory of participating physicians in over 100 cities and more than 55 countries.

The Directory also contains a Personal Medical Data section, where the member should fill in appropriate information such as immunizations, emergency data, etc.

The address:

      Intermedic, Inc.

      777 Third Avenue

      New York, New York 10017

There is also another group called IAMAT, which is the International Association for Medical Assistance to Travelers. This Association has 140 offices operating 24 hours a day in more than 50 countries. Membership cards may be obtained free of charge from a travel agent or from offices of the association at 745 Fifth Avenue, New York, New York 10022.

In most countries in the world one is usually well advised to seek the nearest medical school hospital or university hospital. There the physicians are likely to be the best trained in the country, and the facilities are likely to be adequately equipped with necessary diagnostic facilities and staffed with many required consultants. The better hotels will have available qualified physicians. If you need a physician in an emergency overseas, the American Consulate can recommend one who is qualified. One should also check with their hospital insurance coverage before going overseas.

Most major companies will cover illness and hospitalization in foreign countries. Blue Shield and Blue Cross will reimburse members for the cost of care anywhere in the world if a properly receipted bill is submitted. If you have Blue Shield coverage, take along the proper application blanks so that any physician providing reimbursable service may certify it with his signature. If you have another insurance carrier, check its provisions for overseas coverage and take along appropriate application blanks.

Drinking Water

Be careful with *drinking water* overseas! Even brushing the teeth with tap water can be hazardous. The local people of many countries seem to be resistant to some of the infections transmitted by water. In general, you should consider all tap water potentially hazardous. Bottled water, both carbonated and noncarbonated, is available in most cities and is safe to use. Some of the well-known bottled waters in Europe are those of Perrier, Vichy, Solares, and Evian. Drinking tea and coffee is usually safe, because the water is boiled. In most areas, be cautious in using ice cubes and shaved ice. Ordinarily water can be sterilized by boiling for three to five minutes. Glasses and cups that are used also should be rinsed out with boiling water whenever possible.

If you cannot boil water, then tablets such as Halazone or Globaline should be used. Directions are on the package. One handy trick is to take along tincture of iodine, the kind used on cuts and scratches. A drop or two in a glass of water, or three or four drops in a quart of water, will insure pure water after thirty minutes. This is a simple, uncomplicated, and virtually fool-proof technique. The water may taste a little of iodine, but then that is better than acute dysentery. Often travelers are reluctant to be fussy or to complain about their drinking water in fear of embarrassing their hosts. This is usually unnecessary; the sophisticated host will recognize that there may be some dangers for a newcomer.

Some useful rules of thumb for water:

1. If you do not know for sure that it is safe— do not drink it.
2. Ice is as dangerous as water.
3. Is the container clean? If it is not, then neither is the water.
4. Brushing your teeth with tap water may increase your time spent in the bathroom.
5. Alcohol does not sterilize untreated water or ice cubes.
6. Tea and coffee are safe—if the water has been boiled.

Common Illness
Upper Respiratory Infections

The same advice given in the country in which you live applies even more overseas. Avoid over-chilling, fatigue, and contact with people who apparently have upper respiratory infections. At the first sign of a cold, bed rest, liquids, aspirin and perhaps an antihistamine might be indicated. Persistent fever, cough or a bad sore throat ordinarily would require the advice of a physician. If you must continue your activities, then you must plan them to allow for rest periods during the day.

Diarrhea

You should practice good hygiene and prevent diarrhea, as outlined previously. Should you be unsuccessful in preventing it, then limit activities even though you are feeling well. Weak tea or clear liquids, bouillon, and dry toast are helpful. If there are cramps, a tincture of paragoric or Lomotil should be used. Most diarrhea is of short duration. However, if there is blood or mucus in the stools, a physician should be consulted.

Allergies

These do not usually present much of a problem. Actually in most parts of the world there is less ragweed than there is in the United States. In addition, you have to be settled for a long period of time in order to become sensitized to the local allergenic products. Itchy eyes, or persistent sneezing call for one of the better known antihistamines, such as tripelennamine or chlorpheneramine. If you are allergic to certain materials in the pillow such as feathers, arrangements should be made with the hotel for substitutions, or you might wish to carry your own pillow.

Insomnia

In strange surroundings, you may have difficulty sleeping. If the room itself is comfortable, with a minimum of noise and good ventilation, there should not be much difficulty. Rather than toss and turn all night, however, taking an appropriate dose of sleeping pills before bedtime, will suffice. If you know that you have a tendency to have insomnia be sure to see your private physician before the trip—and take your sleeping pills along.

Another good sedative is secobarbital as a 100 mg. capsule. This usually does not leave you groggy in the morning. Some people can sleep better if they take a walk before bedtime. Others prefer a glass of milk or a highball or a liqueur. Reading may be helpful. Check the bedside reading lamp on registration and insist on an effective light. On the other hand, if you want to shut out light and noise, eye masks and ear plugs are helpful.

Constipation

We keep talking about diarrhea but there will be times when some, because of the change in toilet habits, may be constipated. Dried fruits such as figs are helpful. Dry bran cereal is also of value. The most important thing is to drink plenty of liquids. There may be a tendency to be afraid, even of the bottled water. This is a mistake. Cut down on tea and milk. If constipation persists, Milk of Magnesia tablets are one of the easiest medications to use. In the hurry and stress of schedules, normal regular habits get suppressed. Most important of all—give plenty of time each day for this function.

Foot Problems

Sightseeing often causes sore feet. Yet your feet are your most essential equipment for successful sightseeing and a good vacation. Shoes should be comfortable and well fitting. The toe nails should be cut square across and cuticles pushed down to prevent infection of the nail beds. Foot powder should be sprinkled liberally in the shoes and between the toes to minimize chances of fungus infection. Of course, socks, stockings, and shoes should be changed daily. After a day of sightseeing soaking the feet will relieve aches and fatigue. Gentle massage is useful, and lying down with a pillow under the knees is restful for aching feet.

When outdoors always wear shoes.

Back Problems

You may not be accustomed to the climbing and walking you will be doing. Also, some hotel beds are not as restful as those at home. If you have chronic back difficulties, you should request the manager to have bed boards placed under the mattress. This arrangement can be made ahead of time. Simple back exercises such as lying on the floor and gently bringing one knee up to the chin, alternately, with the assistance of both hands will help to keep the back muscles stretched. Tub baths are also good for fatigue and relaxing a tired aching or strained back. The important thing is to prevent the back strain by limiting the amount of activities initially to prevent and to condition yourself gradually.

Dental Care

You should bring along dental floss for cleaning between the teeth, plenty of toothpaste or powder and at least one or two extra toothbrushes. Again, you should use bottled or purified water to brush the teeth and rinse the mouth. You may find that the meat eaten overseas is not quite as tenderized as the meats to which you have been accustomed. Be careful with the use of dentures because of this.

General Hygiene

Some general hints on hygiene include the proper use of soap. If you have brought along your own soap, this is not a problem. Some of the soap you will get may be harsher than you are accustomed to at home. Women should pack cleansing cream. Shampoo should be in a plastic bottle. Many of these items are available in pharmacies in the cities you visit.

There are a number of preparations which are prepackaged for cleansing the face and hands. One of these is Wash-'n-Dri, a moist scented, disposable cleaner. These can be purchased in quantity and are easily packed.

An adequate supply of sanitary pads should be packed as well as vaginal deodorant lotion. Tampax tampons are also useful.

In Europe, you will be introduced to the bidet. This is a toilet fixture which is useful in cleaning the perineal area with a stream of warm water.

Experienced travelers will, half humorously, relate their experiences with toilet paper overseas. It comes in various styles—often abrasive and nonabsorbent. Pack toilet tissue flat and take along plenty of packets of facial tissue.

In addition to the above, it will be wise to have an adequate supply of deodorant, body powder, and regular toilet articles and cosmetics.

First Aid

This section is not intended to take the place of a regular First Aid Manual. These are just a few hints:

Nosebleed

- Sit upright (not lying down) with head forward.

- Place a small piece of moist cotton with pressure against the nose. Hold pressure for 3-4 minutes.
- Keep head still for at least 5 minutes more.
- Be careful about blowing nose.

Hemorrhoids

- Avoid constipation.
- Use soft toilet tissue.
- Sit in hot tub twice a day for 15 or 20 minutes.
- Elevate legs with pillow under knees three times daily for about 20 minutes.
- Use anesthetic ointment occasionally for pain.

Fainting

- Loosen collar.
- Get into open air.
- Lower head. May put your head between your knees.
- Ammonia ampule whiffs.

Painful Menstrual Periods

- Proper rest and exercise.
- Correct constipation.
- Heat by hot pad or hot towels.
- Mild sedation, aspirin.

Hangover

- Prevention is the key!
- Plenty of liquids with added salt. Tomato juice is good.
- Antacid tablets and aspirin tablets. Best to take these on retiring from a party and in the morning.
- Munch pretzels or salty crackers on arising.

Toothache

- Aspirin

- Heat. Especially warm mouthwash.
- Oil of cloves.

Foreign Body in Eye

- Do not rub. Let tears wash it out.
- Eye cup with warm water.
- If no relief soon, call a physician.

Sunburn

- Prevent sunburn with a good cream and short, gradual exposure to the sun, 15 minutes at a time at the beginning.
- Analgesic or mild hydrocortisone ointment spray or lotion.

Small amounts of regular First Aid materials would be valuable. These would include:

> Band aids
> Small scissors
> Adhesive tape
> Roller gauze
> Antiseptic cream
> Cotton balls
> Elastic bandage
> Eye drops

10
food abroad

*"Soup and fish explain half
of the emotions of life."*

—Sydney Smith

ONE OF THE DELIGHTS of international travel is to become a gourmet. The world presents many "adventures in good eating," with new foods, new eating customs, and even new utensils.

The choices of food may differ from country to country. In some parts of the world mangoes, guava, and curries will be everyday choices. Nothing is so delicious as a tree-ripened banana or citrus fruit at the peak of tastiness. Many new gourmet delights in an array of combinations await you along with the fun of finding and savoring them.

In order to assure a nutritionally well balanced diet you must select correct combinations of food to provide the nutrients you require. Products which you are used to eating at home may not be in the same abundance abroad, and therefore nutritionally equivalent substitutes will have to be used.

Many countries will have food supplies and food habits like your own country, though the preparation is likely to be at least a little different. The use of meat, poultry, fish, and eggs may be limited by their availability, or by their cost, or by traditional belief and customs. There are many countries where cereals, tubers, and roots make up the greatest share of the typical diet. Fruits and vegetables may not be eaten because they are considered to be unimportant or because it is against local custom to eat them. Of course, religious beliefs or traditional taboos make certain foods unavailable.

There are four food groups which make up a nutritionally balanced diet and which you should strive for in your daily diet abroad. A sound diet includes:

Milk

Children	3 to 4 cups
Teenagers	4 cups
Adults	2 cups

Meat
2 or more servings
or substitute beans, peas, or nuts

Vegetables and Fruits
4 or more servings
including citrus, other fruits and green or yellow vegetables and potatoes.

Cereal and Bread
4 or more servings.

Milk is important but presents a problem. Fresh milk, whole, skim and buttermilk, as well as cheese and ice cream, should NOT be eaten or drunk unless you are absolutely certain it has been made safe—such as by boiling. It is wiser to use dry milk or canned evaporated milk, which is available in all countries and is quite satisfactory. If you cannot get milk then you should increase the daily meat serving to three instead of two.

There is a variety of delectable sources of vitamin C in many countries. Examples are acerola cherry, camucamu, guava, mango, papaya, and pomels. Remember dark green and deep yellow vegetables are the best sources of vitamin A, besides being tasty.

The use of unmilled and unpolished rice is preferable to white rice for nutrients and vitamins, and it also has a more interesting flavor. Rice is one of the world's most important cereals and supplements available animal protein with vegetable protein. In the Orient especially, you should cultivate a taste for rice.

Enjoy eating but protect yourself:
- Be certain that the *water* is safe to drink and that the *food* you eat is safe.
- Remember that wine and beer are safe with meals.
- Be aware that fruits may cause some diarrhea.
- Make certain vegetables have been well cooked.
- Fruits and vegetables which are peeled can be safely eaten raw if they are washed in safe water before peeling.
- Boil fresh milk before drinking. If powdered milk is used, boil the water first or use bottled water.
- All meats should be cooked to the well-done stage before eating; be aware of rare meat.
- When in doubt, remember: toast, hot soup, hard-boiled eggs are usually safe.

11 the golden years traveller

> "*Grow old along with me!*
> *The best is yet to be.*"
> —Browning

THE GOLDEN YEARS CAN BE the golden age for travel. Normally healthy people in their later years should not only experience little difficulty in trans-ocean travel, whether by sea or air, but it can be a definite benefit. Away from the demands of the telephone, the desk, or the kitchen sink, perhaps for the first time, the senior citizen can experience through travel a positive lift to the spirit.

The older traveler has acquired the maturity to evaluate new places and new people and their ways. If he is content to be, at times, the prudent observer and not plunge into a timetable of activities abroad which he would never think of following at home, he should be able to add considerably to his enjoyment of life.

The senior citizen whose travel has hitherto been confined to his own country might feel hesitant about traveling on his own. There is no need to worry about that. Tourism today is so much a part of the economy of many countries—especially of those one would naturally wish to visit—that the most modern and efficient modes of travel and accommodation are at every traveler's disposal.

If one is reluctant to travel solely on one's own, the group tour offers an excellent solution. When one travels with a group, practically all the bothersomeness of foreign travel is dispensed with. Transportation to one's hotel, the handling of baggage, tickets to events one wants to see—all these are the province of the tour guide. One's own time and energies can be devoted solely to having a good time and making friends.

The group tour offers the older traveler the presence of congenial but unobtrusive company, and it offers as well, it should be stressed, ample opportunity for leisure time. The group is given an orientation tour, let us say, of the principal sights of London and then is usually given a full day at leisure and an afternoon and evening or two in the same city. This gives the traveler time to rest, or to visit museums and historic places at his own pace. It is a good idea to carry one's flight bag—here's the place for selected items from the medical kit described earlier —with you at all times. Your suitcase, limited to 44 pounds in weight, is something you see only in your hotel room; your tour guide gets it to your room and whisks it away.

Senior citizens today have more time and money to travel than ever before. With the life expectancy in the many countries now close to 70 years for men and 75 years for women, more and more older people will travel. In general, all things being equal, there is no problem except the usual precautions one would take when traveling in his own country.

The elderly make some of the best travelers in the world. Naturally, often the fact they are senior citizens means they have taken good care of themselves. Most of them should and will avoid excesses of food, drink, and exertion.

12 the handicapped traveller

"To know a foreign country at all you must not only have lived in it and your own, but also lived in at least one other."

—Somerset Maugham

IT IS REASSURING TO KNOW that most airlines in this country now prepare their crews to serve the handicapped. As soon as the ticket reservation is made by the airline or through the travel agent, the airlines begin their work of "tagging" the handicapped traveler. For example, seeing-eye dogs may travel free of charge with blind passengers. The dogs must be muzzled, however. All major airport facilities have wheelchairs available for transporting the disabled and a device known as a forklift which can elevate and lower the wheelchair or passenger on a stretcher to the aircraft. All airliners are equipped with complete first aid items and oxygen. There are several travel agents across the country who specialize in booking tours for handicapped people. It is reassuring to know that all flight personnel have had a complete Red Cross course in first aid. For example, the stewardesses get training in artificial cardiac massage, the application of splints and tourniquets, and are trained to deliver babies. Special seating accommodations can be arranged for the handicapped.

In general, then, the airlines make great effort to ensure the handicapped person is given full consideration during travel.

Cardiovascular Problems

Patients with mild cardiovascular disease usually will do well during travel. Most airline physicians will not allow those with congestive heart failure or mild heart attack occurring less than eight to six weeks before departure to travel. Chest pain, if controlled by medication, is no concern usually. The private physician may wish to call the airline officials to discuss his patient with heart disease.

It is also important for the person with heart disease or hypertension to make sure that he has ample supplies of medication prior to the departure. If special laboratory tests are needed, the major cities of the world have laboratories which are equipped with such things as prothrombin tests and other specific laboratory tests.

Lung Disease

An individual with active pulmonary tuberculosis will ordinarily not be cleared for travel on public carriers. Patients with severe emphysema, asthma or lung cancer should, of course, be given special consideration by their physicians before travel.

With planes pressurized as they are, more and more people who have had lung conditions are able to travel. We remember an interesting travel companion we had once on a flight from Frankfurt to Amsterdam who was very proud of the fact that he had been living a normal, comfortable life during the past five years after excision of most of his right lung for cancer. As we sped silently in the small jet, we could not help but marvel at the age in which we live and the ease with which our handicapped and aged can be so mobile and so comfortable.

Diabetes

A well controlled diabetic who understands his condition, diet, and use of insulin will usually have no trouble flying or traveling. The patient with diabetes should have ample supply of his required oral tablets for the duration of the journey. Most oral medication for diabetes, however, is available in overseas areas. The patient with diabetes traveling should also have candy bars immediately available. It is easy to get insulin overseas, and it is preferable to do this because of the refrigeration problem. Disposable syringes and needles are very helpful for the diabetic traveler. Clinistix paper and tablets by the Ames Company are essential for checking urine.

13 traveling with children

"In America there are two classes of travel—first class, and with children."

—Robert Benchley

WITH GOOD PREPARATION, much of the past difficulties in traveling with children can be minimized. The travel agent, the airlines, ships, trains, and buses make great efforts to ease the handling of infants and children. Would that their careful preparation could be matched by the parents themselves!

The first thing to do is have the pediatrician or family physician examine the child, get all needed immunizations up to date, and counsel the parents on the trip.

Infants and children are good travelers. Before departure, adjust the baby's schedule so that irritability and fatigue are kept to a minimum during the trip. It is wise to avoid all stimulation prior to the flight. This means that grandparents and other relatives should be advised to say farewells the day before the trip.

It is wise to take along a supply of powdered milk and any necessary vitamins. The latter are stable even in the liquid form but should be tightly sealed. Disposable bottles are good. The airline and ship will be able to meet most of the feeding needs, such as heating bottles, etc.

We also advise you to carry some small packages of dry cereal. These can be crushed for infants. Older children can usually eat them out of the package, dry, or with milk. For those beyond infancy, pretzels, raisins, and baby franks in jars are excellent.

The stewardess will usually make every effort to see that the baby is able to stretch out. This can be done best by removing the arm rests in unoccupied seats. Extra pillows and blankets are available.

Disposable diapers are especially worthwhile. Take along an adequate supply; it will be difficult to match your brand overseas. The usual ointments, powders, etc., are available overseas.

Most hotels, especially in Europe, have registered babysitters, as do many airline terminals. This service is well developed on board ships.

Relax and remember that the stewards and stewardesses on planes and ships are delighted to have babies on board. You may even get more attention than you need. Night flights are convenient for long journeys with children.

14
traveling
with pets

*"When I play with my cat, who knows but that
she regards me more as a plaything than I do her?"*
— Michel de Montaigne

TRAVEL REGULATIONS FOR PETS vary from country
to country. Some countries require rabies certificates.
Others request health certificates. Many have quarantine rules.

An excellent list of regulations for dogs and cats
traveling abroad has been compiled by the ASPCA
(American Society For the Prevention of Cruelty to
Animals) entitled "Traveling with your Pet."

Some of the advice given for shipping pets by
air are the following:

• A health certificate and a rabies inoculation are
recommended, along with distemper and hepatitis
inoculations.

• Provide a large enough, sturdy crate with a leak-
proof bottom. Print on it your name, address, pet's
name and destination.

• Exercise well on day before shipment.

- Feed a light meal six hours before shipping.
- Don't give water to pet within two hours of shipping except on a very hot day. Provide a water dish for attendant's use.
- If trip will take over 24 hours, provide food.

The following tabulation summarizes some of the regulations for taking pets into foreign countries:

BAHAMAS

Rabies vaccination is required not less than ten days nor more than nine months before departure for the Bahamas. Health certificate signed by a veterinarian must be not more than 24 hours before departure. Dogs and cats under six months of age are admitted only if the owner has obtained a permit from the Bahamas Ministry of Out Island Affairs, Agriculture and Fisheries, at Nassau.

BERMUDA

Import permit must be obtained from the Director of the Department of Agriculture and Fisheries, Point Finger Road, Paget, Bermuda. Applications must be received at least 10 days before the intended date of arrival. Animals without permit will be refused entry.

BRAZIL

Rabies vaccination and health certificate issued by a licensed veterinarian required. Certificates must be certified by the Brazilian Consulate.

CANADA

No restrictions for entry of cats. Dogs must be accompanied by a certificate signed by a licensed veterinarian certifying that the dog has been vaccinated against rabies during the preceding 12 months.

COLOMBIA

Rabies and distemper inoculations required as well as health certificates stating that the dog is free of hepatitis, internal, and external parasites and is in general good health.

FRANCE

Vaccination against rabies is required more than one month and less than six months before entry. A certificate of health delivered no more than three days before departure is acceptable stating the animal comes from a country free of rabies for at least three years and has lived in the country for the last six months (or since birth).

GERMANY (WEST GERMANY AND WEST BERLIN)

No restrictions for cats. For dogs a special permit must be obtained in advance from the one of the ten states of West Germany in which the point of entry is located.

GREAT BRITAIN

Quarantine of six calendar months in approved kennels required for both dogs and cats. Accommodations must be secured at one of the approved quarantine kennels and an authorized carrying agent must be engaged to meet the animal, clear it through customs, and deliver it to the quarantine kennels.

IRELAND

Six-month quarantine for dogs and cats at an approved quarantine kennel. Animal must be transported from the port of entry to the quarantine kennel by an approved carrying agent.

ISRAEL

Rabies inoculation and health certificate signed by a veterinarian are necessary.

ITALY

Certificate of origin and health signed by a veterinarian stating that the animal comes from a locality free of rabies for six months is required. Animal will be examined on entry.

JAMAICA

No dogs or cats admitted, except for animals coming directly from Great Britain, Northern Ireland, or the Republic of Eire.

JAPAN

Dogs: Two-week quarantine. Health certificate and rabies inoculation certificate (at least one month old, but not older than 150 days) necessary.

Cats: One-day quarantine.

MEXICO

Inoculations against rabies and distemper required. Health certificate in duplicate must be dated, bear the owner's name and address, a full description of the animal and tag number, and attest that it has been examined (giving date) and found free of any contagious disease as well as immunized (giving date).

PUERTO RICO

Health certificate, dated not more than 10 days before departure, stating animal is free of disease. Rabies vaccination certificate dated not more than 30 days before departure.

SPAIN

Health and rabies certificates issued by the nearest Spanish Consulate Office.

SWITZERLAND

Rabies vaccination not less than 30 days or more than one year before entry.

THAILAND

Rabies vaccination.

VIETNAM

Send a letter describing pets, expected date and time of arrival, the name of the airline and flight number to the Animal Protection Service, Department of Agriculture, 29 Phan Dinh Phung Street, Saigon, Vietnam (Tel: 91745).

Enclose a health certificate issued not less than 15 days or more than one year before departure, stating that the pet has been vaccinated against rabies (specify type of vaccine used), is in good health and comes from an area free from rabies for more than six months, and is located more than 12.5 miles from a rabies-affected area.

VIRGIN ISLANDS

Health certificate signed by a veterinarian stating that the animal is free from symptoms of infectious, contagious, or communicable disease and did not originate in an area under quarantine for rabies. Dogs and cats more than eight weeks of age must have been vaccinated against rabies within six months or not less than two weeks before shipment and must arrive with proper identification tag and certificate of rabies vaccination.

15
advice
to the
ladies

"Nature is in earnest when she makes a woman."
—Oliver Wendell Holmes

TRAVELING ABROAD SHOULD BE FUN. Therefore, it is most important that you start enjoying your trip while still in the planning stage.

Women may have certain anxieties such as mode of travel, leaving the children behind, possible illness, etc. Relax, use common sense, and take whatever preventive precautions are possible.

Any mode of travel involves long periods of sitting. To insure good circulation, take off your girdle. Girdles have been known to cause many alarms. A few years ago a major airline pilot had to make an emergency landing when a lady passenger developed all the symptoms of appendicitis, which promptly disappeared when her girdle was removed at the hospital. Try substituting a garter belt and the lightweight elasticized panties. It would be better to wear panty hose.

Feminine hygiene, always of extreme importance, should be especially so when traveling abroad. General hygiene and general health hints are outlined throughout this book. However, as a woman, you will have questions and thoughts of your own. First, what should you include in your travel case? Let's start at the top and go from head to toe.

Hair or *scalp* problems? Take along an adequate supply of that special shampoo you use. You may not be able to find it overseas. Women all over the world have their favorite hairdresser, and you will find these inexpensive. Sanitary law may be non-existent, except perhaps in the large cosmopolitan cities. Don't feel embarrassed to take along your own comb and brush when you go to the hairdresser. In the Orient you will be especially pleased to have the young apprentices massage your neck, upper back, and arms while you are under the dryer.

Be sure to take along a small bottle of eyedrops for any foreign matter you might pick up, or just to soothe the eyes after a long day in the sun.

Pack an extra toothbrush. In certain parts of the world it is wise to boil all your drinking water. Keep a bottle in the bathroom for brushing your teeth.

If you will be in a very cold climate, you will need a good face cream for protection against dryness and chapped skin. For extremely hot weather take along disposable medicated face wipes, such as Zepheranchloride Towelettes. These are extremely good for minor skin irritations caused from perspiration. Also, they will take up very little room in your travel case.

If you are a nursing mother, take along cocoa butter soap to aid in preventing cracked and tender nipples. Also, don't be embarrassed about nursing your baby, if you find yourself in an impossible situation. Europeans and Asians, as well as all the other peoples of the world, think nothing of it.

Better take along an ample supply of your favorite deodorant. This is not a best seller in some foreign countries.

In Europe, there is that wonderful invention called the bidet. It is amazing the number of American women who are actually too embarrassed to inquire about its proper function and end up using them for goldfish bowls, flower arrangements and even in some cases for their card trays. These bidets can be filled with warm water and used for bathing purposes. If you are a hemorrhoid sufferer, it is the perfect "sitz" bath. For feminine hygiene there is a fine spray and you will find when there is just no time for a hot leisurely bath, cleansing with a medicated vaginal disposable wipe, such as Tucks, followed by the spray is a wonderful substitute.

Douching for some women is a factor in personal hygiene. However, you know of course that your personal physician or gynecologist should be consulted about this procedure. It's advisable to boil the water while abroad.

Sanitary napkins might be difficult to find in developing countries. If you are living abroad, a catalogue from Sears & Roebuck or Montgomery Ward is a must for such hard-to-get items. They will send these scarce items to you by airmail. If you are on a short journey, take along an ample supply of sanitary napkins. Throw away the box and wrap two or three in a plastic sandwich bag. You will be surprised how many of these you can tuck in all the little spaces and corners of your bag and will lessen the weight as well. If you prefer any of the tampons, again, take an adequate supply. It is not impossible to find these in most of the major cities abroad, but it is better to be prepared.

Low-heeled shoes are a must. Any popular brand of foot powder will prevent your feet from burning and itching after a long day of hopping from cathedral to museum.

In most of the countries of the Orient, toilet facilities are somewhat different from those in other parts of the world. Commodes may be sunken, and it may be necessary to straddle and squat.

If you are on anti-fertility pills, it is assumed you will take along an adequate supply. On the other hand, if you will be living overseas for sometime, you should arrange with your physician to see that you receive them periodically and always by airmail. Surface mail may take six to eight weeks, and by that time you may not have any need for them. These are now available in most major cities of the world.

Before your departure, it is advisable to have a physical checkup and make certain you have all the immunizations necessary for that part of the world in which you will be travelling.

This comment has been based on the age-old premise that an ounce of prevention (and a bit of factual information) is worth a pound of cure. Travel in good health!

16 sports and health overseas

"If you watch a game it's fun. If you play it, it's recreation. If you work at it, it's golf."

—Bob Hope

OVERSEAS, EVERYONE IS A PANCHO SEGURA or a Patsy McCormick. There is a great temptation to undertake activities never attempted at home. This can be hazardous as seen by the number of "Charley horses," twisted ankles, and worse, which come in the wake of the Great American Sportsman overseas.

Golf

This is a favorite. Again, not 36 holes at one crack! Many of the courses in Europe are longer and more arduous. If golfing in Thailand, remember the heat and humidity. Mexico City's altitude must be considered. Of all the sports overseas, this is one of the favorites.

Swimming

Watch the undertow. Use plenty of suntan cream or lotion. In the tropics, watch for barracuda, sharks, and, of course, the dangerous pirhana of Central South America. Remember the usual precautions of over-eating and drinking prior to swimming. Sand gnats and fleas may be bothersome. Body repellent lotion may be useful. Always swim close to shore and with a companion. Make sure the children have adequate supervision and plenty of rest periods.

Tennis

Remember the heat, humidity, and altitude. But most of all, remember your age!

Mountain Climbing

This is for the very fit, trained, and experienced. High altitude mountaineering involves multiple stresses: height, cold, weather, sharp rocks, to mention a few. Slipping on wet rocks and ice causes many accidents in mountain climbing. Various types of cold exposure, especially frostbite, are ever present dangers. "Small mountain" or hill climbing can also have hazards and middle-aged Mr. Sedentary Businessman had better be in A-1 top condition before trying very much of it.

Skiing and Skating

One has to be in good shape to partake of both of these winter sports. Experienced skiers and skaters will probably want to bring their own equipment. Those out for a lark are likely to end up in embarassing difficulty. Many American tourists who do not seem to know any better, pay many orthopedic bills overseas.

Scuba Diving

Scuba diving, snorkeling, and water skiing are becoming very popular sports. The accident rate is high in these activities; it includes such nice little items as speargun wounds, suction and blast injuries, gas-expansion injuries, decompression sickness, and others. Again, these activities are for the trained and the experienced.

The above are only a few of the sports activities and the necessary cautions to be taken. We have not mentioned horseback riding, fishing (which is very good and safe, usually), boating, bowling, and a host of others.

Simple calisthenics and daily walking are excellent means for keeping in shape and help burn up the excess calories. Golf, swimming, and fishing are excellent sports which hold a minimum of health hazards for the overseas traveler.

17 camping abroad

"Love rules the court, the camp, the grove."
—Sir Walter Scott

CAMPING IS BECOMING increasingly popular, especially in Europe, where there are over 10,000 facilities for camping. Most of these facilities have been built within the last five years, so that the sanitary conditions, water supplies, and toilet facilities are very good. Indeed, many of the sites have sophisticated luxury-type items available, such as one near Venice, which has a perfume shop. A number of the larger camping sites have medical and first aid facilities. Most are close to cities.

An excellent guide is available ("Camping Guide to Europe," Paul Lippman, Holt, Rinehart and Winston, New York, 1968).

The following points are worth mentioning for those intending to camp:

• *Type of vehicle.* One of the most convenient, comfortable and safest methods is the use of a camper bus, especially the Volkswagen. Many Americans order these in the States for overseas purchase. For family camping, a camper larger than the Volkswagen may be necessary.

The Volkswagen camper is wired like a trailer house, with a rear outside plug and two inside outlets, which affords more permanent quarters in winter and summer. A small electric heater may be used inside.

Other types of vehicles such as our caravan-type trailer are used widely, but they offer some difficulties especially since the roads will not always be as wide or as good as those at home. Europeans mostly use 13-16 foot caravans.

Many younger people will get around by motorcycle or bicycle in order to take advantage of the camping grounds.

Licenses for motor bikes are not difficult to obtain, but one should acquire some instruction and skill before venturing into the European traffic. Anyone who has visited Bermuda at Easter is well acquainted with the swarms of American college students who take to motor bikes for the first time without adequate instruction or practice. The accident rate is very high.

• *Drinking water*. While most European camping facilities have safe water supplies, campers should boil drinking water or use purification tablets. Water for brushing the teeth should also be boiled or purified. Many of the camp sites will have bottled mineral water, bottled soft drinks, and beer, which are usually safe.

• *"Native" foods*. There are many temptations to take advantage of the extraordinary cuisine of some of the smaller towns and villages, especially in France. Care must be taken, especially since refrigeration is not a feature of many of these quaint places. Please see comment on these precautions in other sections of this book.

• *Toilet facilities.* These are generally good. Usually you must supply your own soap and toilet tissue.

• *Fatigue.* Touring and camping can be very tiring especially for the driver or the cyclist. An upper limit of 200 miles a day is even probably too much.

18 the health resort

"To be sick is to enjoy monarchal prerogatives."
—Charles Lamb

IN THE COURSE OF YOUR TRAVELS you may be visiting or staying at a health resort or spa. Today the spa is less often patronized than in former years when many spas were famous sites for health promotion and rejuvenation. In the United States, Saratoga Springs, New York, and Hot Springs, Arkansas, are famous health resorts; in Europe, Baden-Baden and Bad Nuheim come to mind. In Europe there have been spas since the time of the ancient Greeks. Pliny, in his *Natural History*, devotes a special chapter to the use of mineral waters. In Europe there are medical specialists who devote their practice to the medicinal use of baths and mineral springs. These practitioners are called balneologists.

Mineral springs have attracted sick people for centurieş on account of the taste, smell, color, and temperature of the water. In terms of today's medical knowledge we know that the basic therapeutic value of the spa lies in physical medicine and hydrotherapy and that there are no special or peculiar healing qualities, per se, in the water of a particular spa.

Certainly, individuals with chronic musculo-skeletal disorders such as arthritis, low-back syndrome, or chronic aches and pains can be helped by the spa. Also, if the spa has a general health program which emphasizes physical fitness and dieting, most middle-aged people, and even some not so middle-aged, can profit very much from such a regime.

More and more scientific data is being collected which indicates that obesity, lack of physical fitness and exercise, and cigarette smoking are the most important factors contributing to premature heart attacks, and chronic pulmonary problems. If a health resort or spa teaches you good health habits and restores muscle tone as well as reducing a flabby girth, then it is probably well worth the investment.

You must be cautious of medical quackery and charlatanism associated with the health resort. Beware of institutions that make claims and print testimonials. A good institution should have competent medical supervision and have suitable clinical and physical facilities.

You should discuss with your personal physician the advisability or usefulness of visiting a health resort. If he can recommend it for you and can make arrangements for you with the medical director, then indeed it can be a very useful experience. This procedure will protect you from any quakery which might be associated with some institutions. The experience can be a truly recreational vacation.

19 health hints for three well traveled areas:

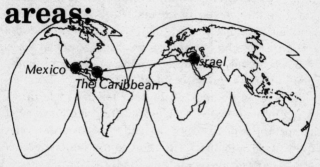

"A good traveler is one who does not know where he is going to, and a perfect traveler does not know where he came from."

—Lin Yutang

MEXICO

TRAVELERS ARE FINDING THAT MEXICO offers many attractions: a good climate, Aztec and Mayan temples, the glamour of Mexico City, and a Spanish culture, with diversified sports and shopping opportunities.

The main entry to Mexico is the air route. Some people drive and others go by bus or train.

The following hints may be of value.

"Turista" (Montezuma's Revenge)

Diarrhea is a vastly overrated problem. Some of it is psychological. Again, the precautions listed in other parts of this book prevail. In metropolitan areas: Mexico City, Guadalajara, etc., there is usually no difficulty with the drinking water if you are staying at the reliable hotels and eating at recommended restaurants. When in doubt, use bottled water. Mexican beer is excellent.

One should be careful about salads and raw fruit and vegetables. True Mexican food is usually not as spicy as that served in border towns or Los Angeles and San Antonio.

Outside the Metropolitan areas, special care should be taken about drinking water, ice cubes, and raw fruits and vegetables.

There is no real proof that taking single drugs or combinations will prevent diarrhea. The most important aspects are a relaxed state of mind, adequate rest, and strict attention to the sanitary points above, concerning water and food.

Altitude

Mexico City has an altitude of 7,347 feet. Visitors will notice that with exertion (rapid walking, running or walking up an incline) there is a slight shortness of breath. This is nothing to worry about if you are in good physical condition. This shortness of breath disappears after a few days. Anyone with a heart or lung condition should take extra precautions.

Physicians and Hospitals

The cities have excellent physicians and hospitals. Many of the doctors travel and study in the United States. Mexico City and Guadalajara are medical centers. Pharmacies are well stocked with most American products.

General Items

- A smallpox certificate is no longer necessary for American citizens returning to the United States.

- Recommendations for typhoid shots may be made for certain parts of Mexico.
- Water sports and sunbathing are favorite past-times. Be careful about sunburn.

THE CARIBBEAN

North American travelers are becoming more interested in traveling to the Caribbean. Travel there is easy with frequent inexpensive air and steamship trips.

The climate is, of course, the major attraction. It provides an excellent opportunity for outdoor sports: swimming, fishing, boating, and golfing.

There are some general points to remember:

Sun Bathing

It is very easy to overdo this. Gradual exposure, adequate head and body cover, and protective creams are essential.

Drinking Water

In general, while staying at resort hotels it is safe to drink the water and milk. In rural areas it would be best to boil the water or drink bottled water.

Sports

Water skiing, scuba diving, and boating are popular sports in the Caribbean. One should not participate in these activities unless there has been adequate preparation, practice, and conditioning.

In the middle of the day, temperature and humidity makes strenuous sports such as tennis prohibitive. Again, one should be in good condition for these activities.

	Availability of Physicians	Hospitals	Drugs and Supplies	Sanitation	Other
BARBADOS	MDs and Dentists available	Adequate for uncomplicated cases	Most are available	Pure drinking water Milk pasteurized	
BERMUDA	MDs and Dentists available	Adequate for uncomplicated cases (Hamilton)	Most are available	Pure drinking water Milk pasteurized Food shopping same as USA	
HAITI	MDs and Dentists available Older equipment	Not very adequate	Many are available	Good bottled water Boil tap water Boil local milk	
JAMAICA	MDs and Dentists available	Adequate (Kingston)	Most are available	Boil water in rural areas Pasteurized milk available	Kingston has med. school
BAHAMAS	MDs and Dentists available	Adequate (Nassau)	Most are available	Pure drinking water Milk is imported	
PUERTO RICO	MDs and Dentists available	Adequate	Most are available	Pure drinking water except in rural areas Milk pasteurized	Medical school in San Juan
TRINIDAD	MDs and Dentists available	Adequate for uncomplicated cases	Many are available	Water is O.K. in resort hotels Powdered or evap. milk available	
U. S. VIRGIN ISLANDS	MDs and Dentists available	Adequate (St. Thomas)	Most are available	Water is O.K. Milk pasteurized	

ISRAEL

One of the favorite journeys for North Americans is to Israel. It has a delightful Mediterranean climate, with an especially pleasant climate during spring and fall. The summers are hot and the winters rainy. During spring, beginning in March, from time to time a khamsin or sharar blows through. It is a hot dry wind and the humidity drops precipitously. The health hazards of Israel are minor. There may be initially some upset stomachs and diarrhea. Prudent diets and the careful washing of fruits and vegetables is advised. The tap water in Israel, while high in mineral content, which by the way may cause diarrhea initially, is safe for drinking. Bottled sterilized, pasteurized milk is available.

The warm Mediterranean climate is ideal for wash and wear clothing. The winter can be quite cool and damp, though, and you will find that sweaters, socks, warm underwear, and warm night clothing are desirable. A coat will be required during this season.

Health care in Israel is excellent. It has the highest doctor to patient ratio in the world and there are several world famous medical institutions, especially the Hadassah University Hospital.

20
special precautions: the tropics

"*There passed a weary time. Each throat was parched, and glazed each eye.*"
—Coleridge, *Rime of the Ancient Mariner*

"*Joy and Temperance and Repose*
Slam the door on the doctor's nose."
—Longfellow

THERE IS AN EXCELLENT PAMPHLET called "Health Hints for the Tropics." (See references.)

Dress comfortably. Loose fitting clothes that will wash easily are the best. They should be changed frequently. Wear shoes at all times because of the ease of picking up hookworm and stongyloides which have reached invasive larval stages while maturing in the soil. There are some tropical vegetations which can cause contact dermatitis. If one is going to be in the sun for any length of time, he should wear some kind of a protective head covering. In addition, exertion and perspiring will cause a salt loss. Extra

100

salt may be taken in food or take supplementary salt tablets, when necessary. It is important to get a noon siesta each day in the tropics especially until you are acclimated.

Be careful about long exposure to the sun. Wear a hat. Sun glasses are a must. Some may want to use protective face creams part of the time and special lipstick. Special creams for the skin should be applied every three or four hours during exposure and reapplied after swimming. Before setting out on hiking expeditions or camping, one should take into consideration any dangers of snakes. Dangerous land snakes may be found in many parts of the world. It is best to make local inquiry about this. Scorpion stings may be a problem. If camping out be sure to inspect sleeping bags, clothing, and shoes before using.

Other considerations for travel in the tropics are the following:

Insect Repellent

There is a liquid called "OFF" which is very effective. Another good one is an insect repellent stick called "6-12" by Carbide Chemicals of New York. Be careful of contact dermititis. Test over a small skin area first. Some campers also like to use an Aerosol "bomb" as a space sprayer to clear a wide area. Keep these products away from the eyes.

Snake Bite Kit

These will usually be available, but a cautious traveler may wish to check ahead of time.

Prickly Heat

This is always a problem in the tropics. It is most important to wear light, loose clothing to give maximum ventilation. Bathe and wash frequently. Use a medicated body powder. Calamine Lotion is helpful.

Heat Exhaustion, Sunstroke

Excessive sun bathing is unwise. Drink large quantities of liquids. Take salt additives if required for heavy perspiration.

Early symptoms are dizziness, faintness, headache, blurring of vision, and sometimes nausea and vomiting. Wear a hat of some type and take a mid-day siesta. Remember what is said about "only mad dogs and Englishmen stay out in the mid-day sun." There are many others who do not use good sense in this regard.

Travelers intending long stays in the tropics should avail themselves of some of the additional publications listed on page 113.

The Mosquito

Almost all mosquitoes require blood meals to reproduce. In so doing, they often ingest viruses or parasites from sick humans or animals. These parasites in turn are transmitted to healthy individuals when the mosquitoes take a subsequent blood meal. There are a number of important diseases transmitted by various species of mosquitoes.

Human malaria is transmitted only by the female Anopheles mosquito. Man is susceptible to four species of malaria parasites. This disease has wide distribution in mild climates of the world. The World Health Organization has done a remarkable job in the past decade in removing some of the threat of malaria.

Malaria

In order to prevent malaria, it is necessary to take malaria suppressive drugs. The drug of choice for the prevention of suppressing malaria is generally called chloroquin phosphate. Trade names are Aralen, Nivaquine B, and Resochin. There are others your physician may wish to prescribe. Suppressive treatment should be started before traveling. See page 32.

Yellow Fever

This disease is present in reservoir animals such as monkeys. It is transmitted by a mosquito, the Aedes Egypti. There is no specific drug for it. Fortunately the traveler can be fully protected against yellow fever by yellow fever vaccine. Yellow fever is present in South America and Africa.

Filariasis

The term filariasis refers to a group of microscopic wormlike parasites which dwell in the lymphatic system and blood stream. These parasites are transmitted by a variety of blood-sucking insect carriers. In Africa, there are two kinds of filariasis. Loa Loa is transmitted through the bite of a mangrove fly in certain parts of equatorial Africa. Onchoceriasis, another type of filariasis, occurs in Africa and tropical America. It is transmitted by the black gnat. In the Pacific and Asia there are several types of blood filaria transmitted by a variety of mosquitoes.

The best protection is to use insect repellent, wear long sleeved clothing, have proper screening, and employ mosquito netting. One may use a drug called Hetrazan (Banocide) as a prophylaxis. Upon a traveler's return from an infected area, he should be checked so that proper treatment may be given if required.

Chagas Disease

Although usually restricted to South America, several cases have been reported from Texas. It is transmitted by the "Barbiero" or "kissing bug." There is no drug or vaccine for this. Travelers on vacation staying in the larger cities will not usually have this problem. Those on extended tours in South America, especially in rural areas, should check in with local public health authorities to assess the problem and the preventive measures.

Schistosomiasis

The schistosome is a small bloodworm or fluke, which causes a disease called schistosomiasis or bilharzia. This disease has a complex life history; it lives in a variety of fresh water snails during part of its life cycle. A free-living stage of the fluke lives in water and is capable of penetrating the unbroken human skin. The fluke after entering the body prefers to live in blood vessels of the intestines, in the liver, and also in the vessels around the bladder, depending upon the particular species of fluke.

Because the fluke lives in fresh water such as lakes and streams, it is very dangerous to wade or swim in unknown waters in many parts of the world. Swimming pools which are filtered and chlorinated are safe. In Africa any natural water is potentially dangerous, for example the Nile and Lake Victoria. In Southeast Asia such as the Phillipines the danger contracting schistosomiasis exists. Sea water is safe, as the fluke dies because of the high salinity. Limit your swimming to swimming pools or the ocean.

Intestinal Parasites

There is a variety of worm-like creatures and amoeba which live in the gastro intestinal tract of higher mammals. Many of these creatures may be looking for a home in you. In order to prevent this from occurring, you must practice scrupulous food hygiene. We have repeatedly stressed the importance of this in relation to what to eat and what not to eat while in underdeveloped areas of the world. These parasites are usually transmitted in uncooked vegetables or meat, and therefore thorough cooking will prevent transmission. Conversely, salads can be eaten only at the risk of providing a home for a lonely parasite. Unfortunately, these organisms often cause grave and serious disease. Any persistent gastro-intestinal symptoms such as pain and diarrhea should be investigated by a physician who can do the required laboratory tests to make a diagnosis.

21 special precautions:

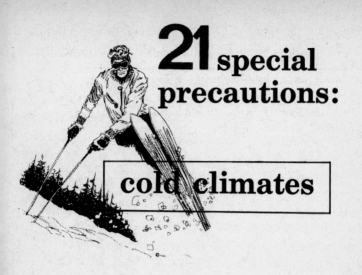

cold climates

"What freezings have I felt, what dark days seen! What old December's bareness every where!"
—Shakespeare

EVEN THOUGH FEW TRAVELERS WILL BE GOING to cold climates for vacation, there are others whose work will take them there. It is interesting to know that almost 20 per cent of the land area of the earth (half of which is in the Soviet Union and Canada) has a mean yearly temperature below zero degrees centigrade. When high winds are added to extremely cold temperatures, the chances of cold injury are increased.

Frostbite is a preventable condition. The traveler who will be in a cold climate for a long period should read the reference article by Washburn listed in the selected references. He cites the danger of exercising or rubbing a frozen part with snow.

Cold climate vacations remind us of the many accidents seen in skating and skiing. Certainly one of the hazards is the skier who is inexperienced or who skies sporadically—the week-end skier. Skiing should only be done if the traveler has the experience and the proper conditioning. It is bad enough breaking an ankle in Colorado, but in the outreaches of the Austrian Alps it could be a major problem.

22 special precautions: high altitudes

"Great things are done when men and mountains meet."

—Blake

AT HIGH ALTITUDES even healthy travelers will often experience some difficulty as their heart and lungs, because of decreased oxygen, work with an output above normal. When normal people add exercise or other exertions to their activities at high altitudes, the work of these organs is increased and placed under considerable stress.

The average person needs about a week or more to adjust to the diminished oxygen tension of high altitudes. The first day or so one might feel a little breathless or experience a slight headache. These symptoms increase with exercise. By the third day most of these symptoms decrease.

If the normal person is affected this way, then, of course, it is easy to see where travelers with certain chronic conditions might have added difficulties.

At 8,000 feet elevation, atmospheric pressure is reduced about 25 per cent.

Travelers with active pulmonary disease or emphysema must be careful. Also travelers with anemia, recent heart attacks, and poorly compensated cardiac valvular disease or hypertension must use great caution.

In general, when visiting or staying in any city with an elevation of 5,000 feet or more, it is wise to spend the first day or so resting in the hotel to become acclimated.

It is wise to eat and drink with great moderation and to have the principal meal at midday. Certainly alcohol consumption should be severely curtailed until after acclimatization, especially at altitudes above 7,500 feet. The atmosphere is thin at these altitudes accompanied by brilliant sunlight. The use of sunglasses and skin protection is well-advised.

We have placed in the Appendix (page 114) the altitude of major cities of the world.

back HOME

"Travel is broadening, particularly where the food and drink are good. But the journey home is an exultant occasion."

—Brooks Atkinson

ONE WHO HAS BEEN in less developed countries for an extended period of time should check in with the physician on return. If the stay has been several months or more, a complete physical examination, including stool, and urine examinations usually should be performed. Travelers returning from certain areas like Africa and the South Pacific should have blood studies for filariasis. Any patient who returns home with symptoms of abdominal cramps and diarrhea needs a complete check-up for intestinal parasites. If the traveler who has returned from parts of the world where malaria is endemic, has an unexplained fever, he should see his physician. Occasionally, a superficial fungus disease such as ringworm will be picked up overseas. One of many different types of fungus could be picked up overseas. Wary travelers will usually not be in trouble.

Again, however, it is important to contact the family physician on return. Symptoms such as persistent fever, abdominal pain, loose stools, skin rashes, persistent cough, or fatigue should be reported at once.

23 questions frequently asked after the trip

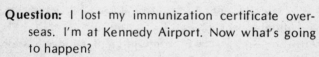

Question: I lost my immunization certificate overseas. I'm at Kennedy Airport. Now what's going to happen?

Answer: Be prepared for a two-week stay in quarantine or to being vaccinated on the spot. And either of these will happen even if you have not lost your certificate but the validity period has lapsed.

Question: My immunizations have expired. Should I retain my immunization certificate?

Answer: By all means. This is a permanent health record and can be revalidated when revaccination is performed.

Question: I contracted malaria while in Thailand. Can it be transmitted to the rest of the family?

Answer: No. Probably not, unless you live in an area abundant in the Anopheles mosquito.

Question: Are there any diseases that I could have contracted on my trip for which there are no obvious early symptoms?

Answer: Yes. That's why we recommend that you have an examination (especially a stool examination) by your physician after your trip.

Question: I have been living in a high-altitude area and now I am in Ecuador and now I'm coming back home to New York City. Is there any problem in this change in altitude?

Answer: No. The readjustment to lower altitudes is easier than the converse (i.e., from Amsterdam to Denver).

Question: I have just returned from an extended stay in the Orient. My next regular check-up is two months away. Should I wait until then?

Answer: No. Get your appointment changed and make your regular check-up now.

Question: I took my pet with me on my trip. Could it have picked up anything that would endanger the family at home?

Answer: We can't be sure. It's best to take your pet to the veterinarian for an examination upon your return.

selected references

Most, Harry, M.D. (Editor), *Health Hints for the Tropics,* American Society of Tropical Medicine and Hygiene, 1964.

Washburn, B., *Travelers' Medical Guide for Physicians,* Kean and Tucker (C. Thomas, Springfield, Ill.) 1966, pp. 363-390, Appendix VII.

A.M.A. First Aid Manual, American Medical Assoc., 535 No. Dearborn Street, Chicago, Illinois.

Pierce, E. B., *New Horizons: Living Abroad.* Pan American's Guide to Living Conditions in 88 Countries. Pan American, P.O. Box 1790, New York 17, New York.

Rule, Colter, *A Traveler's Guide to Good Health.* Garden City, New York, Doubleday and Co., Inc. 1960.

U.S. Dept. of Health, Education and Welfare, *Immunization Information for International Travel.* U.S. Govt. Printing Office, Washington, D.C. 20025.

appendix B

SEASONAL MEAN TEMPERATURES AND ALTITUDES OF PRINCIPAL WORLD CITIES*

	Feb.	May	Aug.	Nov.		Alt.
Middle East						
Israel	48°	67°	76°	58°	Jerusalem	2,500'
Lebanon	57.7	71.8	83.1	67.3	Beirut	25'
Syria	50	70	80	57	Damascus	700'
Turkey	41	63	75	54	Istanbul	30'
Bermuda, Bahamas, and Caribbean						
Jamaica	77	80	82	79	Kingston	25'
Mexico and Central America						
Guatemala	62.8	68	66	62.8		
Mexico	57	67	64	58	Mexico City	4,850'
Panama, C.Z.	80	80	80	78	Panama City	7,349'
						40'
South America						
Argentina	73	55	51	65	Buenos Aires	45'
Bolivia	54	51	49	55	La Paz	12,200'
Brazil	80	72	70	75	Rio de Janeiro	30'
Br. Guiana	79	80	81	81		
Chile	66	55	51	63	Santiago	1,800'
Colombia	58	59	57	58	Bogota	8,500'
Ecuador	55	55	56	55	Quito	9,248'

(Continued)

* Only altitudes of the capital cities are given; it should be noted that nearby resort areas may be considerably higher.

SEASONAL MEAN TEMPERATURES AND ALTITUDES OF PRINCIPAL WORLD CITIES

	Feb.	May	Aug.	Nov.		
South America (Cont'd)						
Fr. Guiana	80	80	82	82	Cayenne	25'
Paraguay	80	67	66	76	Asuncion	253'
Peru	74	67	62	67	Lima	501'
Surinam	80	80	82	82		–
Uruguay	72	57	52	64	Montevideo	30'
Venezuela	67	71	69	69	Caracas	3,164'
Europe						
Austria	34°	58°	65°	39	Vienna	550'
Belgium	38	55	64	43	Brussels	190'
Denmark	32	51	61	40	Copenhagen	25'
England, Wales and N. Ireland	40	54	62	44	London	245'
Finland	22	46	59	32	Helsinki	25'
France	40	57	65	43	Paris	300'
Germany	33	56	63	39	Frankfort	300'
Greece	49	69	81	58	Athens	–
Ireland	41	50	58	44	Dublin	30'
Italy	48	64	76	53	Rome	95'
Luxembourg	38	55	64	43	Brussels	1,200'

(Continued)

SEASONAL MEAN TEMPERATURES AND ALTITUDES OF PRINCIPAL WORLD CITIES

	Feb.	May	Aug.	Nov.		Alt.
Europe (Con'd)						
Majorca (Balearic Is.)	51	66	77	58		4,740' (Max.)
Netherlands	37	54	62	42	Amsterdam	16'
Norway	26	51	60	33	Oslo	40'
Portugal	52	62	72	57	Lisbon	285'
Scotland	39	50	57	42	Glasgow	195'
Spain	44	61	75	47	Madrid	2,150'
Sweden	27	49	60	35	Stockholm	35'
Switzerland	33	56	64	39	Geneva	1,237'
Asia and Philippine Islands						
Burma	75	84	76	75	Rangoon	55'
Indo-China	83	86	82	80		
Hong Kong	59	77	83	70	Hong Kong	25'
India	71	87	84	74	Calcutta	85'
Japan	39	62	79	52	Tokyo	30'
Pakistan	70	84	82	76	Karachi	50'
Philippine Is.	76	82	80	77	Manila	25'
Thailand (Siam)	82	86	84	80	Bangkok	40'
Singapore	81	82	82	81	Singapore	25'

forms used
IN PROCESSING OVERSEAS TRAVELERS
FROM THE GEORGETOWN UNIVERSITY
INTERNATIONAL HEALTH SERVICES CLINIC

GEORGETOWN UNIVERSITY HOSPITAL
INTERNATIONAL HEALTH SERVICES CLINIC

FORM #1   (General Information)

Client's Name   **Sex**

                                  Age

Address

   Home:

   Business:

Referred by:

Countries to be visited:

Duration:

Beginning Date:

Tourist?

Business?

Other?

Ever out of the country before?

Have you ever had or have you now . . . (Please check appropriate answer)

	YES	NO	COMMENTS
Heart trouble			
Lung Disease			
Diabetes			
Nervous Ailments			
Skin Disease			
Allergies			
Are you now in good health?			
Are you undergoing medical treatment now?			
Are you taking any kind of medicine or shots now?			

ALLERGY HISTORY

To be filled in by all clients before specific immunization can be given

	YES	NO	EXPLAIN
Have you ever had any previous reactions to shots?			
Are you allergic to eggs?			
Do you have Eczema? Does anyone in your family have Eczema?			
Do you have any contact skin allergies?			
Have you ever had hay fever or asthma?			
Have you ever taken anti-histamines?			

IMMUNIZATIONS

Date last Series or Boosters	Type Immunization	Clinic M.D. Recomm. (Check)	Date Given (Initials of Nurse)	Date Next Shot Due	Date Next Shot Due	Comments
	Smallpox					
	Tetanus					
	Diphtheria					
	Polio					
	Typhoid-Para Typhoid					
	Typhus					
	Cholera					
	Yellow Fever					
	Plague					
	Measles					
	Whooping Cough					
	Other					

RECOMMENDATIONS TO TRAVELER AND REFERRING PHYSICIAN OR CLINIC

(Excluding Immunization)

Countries Involved

Major Health Hazards

Current New Problems

Medications Recommended

Other Specific Advice

Educational Material Given
  or Recommended

(Signature of Physician).......................

(Date).............................

FOLLOW-UP QUESTIONNAIRE

Please fill this out and return to us in the self-addressed envelope.

Name: ....

Date or Dates seen in Georgetown University International Health Clinic

*   *   *

1) Were your immunizations adequate for your travel?
   Yes ☐ No ☐ Explain:

2) Were there health hazards in the countries you visited we did not tell you about? Yes ☐ No ☐ If Yes, please explain.

3) Did you have any illnesses abroad? Yes ☐ No ☐

   Physician involved:

   Hospital involved:

4) How do you think we could have been of more service to you?

I. INTERNATIONAL CERTIFICATES OF VACCINATION

AS APPROVED BY

THE WORLD HEALTH ORGANIZATION

(EXCEPT FOR ADDRESS OF VACCINATOR)
CERTIFICATS INTERNATIONAUX DE VACCINATION
APPROUVÉS PAR
L'ORGANISATION MONDIALE DE LA SANTÉ
(SAUF L'ADRESSE DU VACCINATEUR)

II. PERSONAL HEALTH HISTORY

TRAVELER'S NAME—Nom du voyageur

JAMES E. BANTA, M.D.

| **ADDRESS** | (Number—Numéro) | (Street—Rue) |
| **ADRESSE** | | |

(City—Ville)

| (County—Département) | (State—État) |

U.S. DEPARTMENT OF
HEALTH, EDUCATION, AND WELFARE

PUBLIC HEALTH SERVICE

PHS-731
Rev. 9-66

READ CAREFULLY
INSTRUCTIONS
Pages 10 and 11

S/N 0108-400-0703

INTERNATIONAL CERTIFICATE OF VACCINATION OR REVACCINATION AGAINST SMALLPOX
CERTIFICAT INTERNATIONAL DE VACCINATION OU DE REVACCINATION CONTRE LA VARIOLE

This is to certify that
Je soussigné(e) certifie que _JAMES E. BANTA, M.D._
whose signature follows
dont la signature suit _James E. Banta_

sex _MALE_
sexe
date of birth _13 Jul 27_
né(e) le

has on the date indicated been vaccinated or revaccinated against smallpox with a freeze-dried or liquid vaccine certified to fulfill the recommended requirements of the World Health Organization.

a été vacciné(e) ou revacciné contre la variole à la date indiquée ci-dessous, avec un vaccin lyophilisé ou liquide certifié conforme aux normes recommandées par l'Organisation mondiale de la Santé.

Date	Show by "X" whether / Indiquer par "X" s'il s'agit de	Signature, professional status, and address of vaccinator / Signature, qualité professionnelle, et adresse du vaccinateur	Origin and batch no. of vaccine / Origine du vaccin et numéro du lot	Approved stamp Cachet d'authentification
1a	Primary vaccination performed / Primovaccination effectuée ☐			
1b	Read as successful Prise ☐ Unsuccessful Pas de prise ☐			
2	_1969_ ✗	_S. J. Doyle, M.D._ INTERNATIONAL HEALTH SERVICES CENTER	_PARKE, DAVIS_	BANTA'S RADIATION CENTER

Revaccination ☐		
Revaccination ☐		
5 Revaccination ☐		

THE VALIDITY OF THIS CERTIFICATE shall extend for a period of 3 years, beginning 8 days after the date of of a successful primary vaccination* or, in the event of a revaccination, on the date of that revaccination.

The approved stamp mentioned above must be in a form prescribed by the health administration of the country in which the vaccination is performed.

Any amendment of this certificate, or erasure, or failure to complete any part of it, may render it invalid.

LA VALIDITÉ DE CERTIFICAT couvre une période de trois ans commençant huit jours après la date de la primovaccination effectuée avec succès (prise) ou, dans le cas d'une revaccination, le jour de cette revaccination.

Le cachet d'authentification doit être conforme au modèle prescrit par l'administration sanitaire du territoire où la vaccination est effectuée.

Toute correction ou rature sur le certificat ou l'omission d'une quelconque des mentions qu'il comporte puet affector sa validité.

* See page 10, item 2.

nation est effectuée. (Aux États Unis ce cachet doit être celui du Service d'Hygiène, de l'état, de la ville ou du comté ou le vaccinateur exerce la médecine, du Département de la Défense, d'un centre désigné de vaccination contre la fièvre jaune, le sceau du Service de la Santé Publique des États Unis, ou le timbre spécial "S-C" approuvé par ce service.)

Toute correction ou rature sur le certificat ou l'omission d'une quelconque des mentions qu'il comporte peut affecter sa validité.

*If unsuccessful, vaccination must be repeated and a new certificate executed.
Si la vaccination n'a pas prise, il faudra recommencer et un nouveau certificat devra être établi.

INTERNATIONAL CERTIFICATE OF VACCINATION OR REVACCINATION AGAINST YELLOW FEVER

CERTIFICAT INTERNATIONAL DE VACCINATION OU DE REVACCINATION CONTRE LA FIÈVRE JAUNE

This is to certify that
Je soussigné(e) certifie que _James Elyan Benta M.D._ sex _Male_ sexe

whose signature follows
dont la signature suit _James E Benta_ date of birth né(e) le _18 July 1927_

has on the date indicated been vaccinated or revaccinated against yellow fever.
a été vacciné(e) ou revacciné(e) contre la fièvre jaune à la date indiquée.

Date	Signature and professional status of vaccinator / Signature et qualité professionnelle du vaccinateur	Origin and batch number of vaccine / Origine du vaccin employé et numéro du lot	Official stamp of vaccinating center / Cachet officiel du centre de vaccination
	O. Roberts, M.D.	National Drug Co.	

U.S. GOVERNMENT PRINTING OFFICE : 1959 O—502836

5520

VACCINATING CENTER	P.H.S. Outpt.
CENTRE DE VACCINATION	4th & C Sts. S.W.
ADDRESS (CITY—VILLE)	Washington, D.C. (STATE—ÉTAT)
ADRESSE	

THIS CERTIFICATE IS VALID only if the vaccine used has been approved by the World Health Organization and if the vaccinating center has been designated by the health administration for the country in which that center is situated.

THE VALIDITY OF THIS CERTIFICATE shall extend for a period of 6 years, beginning 10 days after the date of vaccination (for India, Pakistan, and Ceylon 12 days) or, in the event of a revaccination, within such period of 6 years, from the date of that revaccination.

Any amendment of this certificate, or erasure, or failure to complete any part of it, may render it invalid.

CE CERTIFICAT N'EST VALABLE que si le vaccin employé a été approuvé a l'Organisation Mondiale de la Santé et si le centre de vaccination a été habilité par l'administration sanitaire du territoire dans lequel ce centre est situe.

LA VALIDITÉ DE CE CERTIFICAT couvre une période de six ans commençant dix jours après la date de la vaccination (pour l'Inde, Pakistan et Ceylan 12 jours) ou, dans le cas d'une revaccination au cours de cette période de six ans, le jour de cette revaccination.

Toute correction ou rature sur le certificat ou l'omission d'une quelconque des mentions qu'il comporte peut affecter sa validité.

INTERNATIONAL CERTIFICATE OF VACCINATION OR REVACCINATION AGAINST CHOLERA

CERTIFICAT INTERNATIONAL DE VACCINATION OU DE REVACCINATION CONTRE LE CHOLÉRA

This is to certify that
Je soussigné(e) certifie que _James Elmer Berta M.D._ sex _Male_
sexe

date of birth / _July_
né(e) le _____ _1927_

whose signature follows
dont la signature suit _James E Berta_

has on the date indicated been vaccinated or revaccinated against cholera.
a été vacciné(e) ou revacciné(e) contre le choléra à la date indiquée.

Date	Signature, professional status, and address of vaccinator Signature, qualité professionnelle, et adresse du vaccinateur	Approved stamp Cachet d'authentification
8 JUN 1964	O. Roberts M.D. ½ c.c. Med. Ofcr.,PHS Outp.CL 4th & C Sts.,Washington,D.C.	Booster
8 NOV 1964	W.J. Moore, M.D. MED.OFCR.PHS OUTPT. CL 4TH & C STS.SW, WASHINGTON, DC	½ cc (1 series)
	John M. Lynch, M.D. National Institutes of Health	

1-5824 10cc.

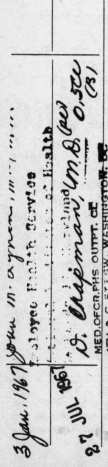

3 Jan. 1967

Employee Health Service

_____ _____ _ Health

27 JUL 1967

D. Chapman, M.D. (s)
(TS)

MED.OFCR.PHS OUTPT. CE

ME.OFCR.PHS WASHINGTON. D.C.

THE VALIDITY OF THIS CERTIFICATE shall extend for a period of 6 months, beginning 6 days after the first injection of the vaccine or, in the event of a revaccination within such period of 6 months on the date of that revaccination. (In the United States two injections are given for the initial series.)

The approved stamp mentioned above must be in a form prescribed by the health administration of the country in which the vaccination is performed. (In the United States, the stamp is that of the local or State health department of the area in which the immunizing-physician practices, the Department of Defense, a designated yellow fever vaccination center, the seal of the Public Health Service, or the special "S–C" stamp approved by the latter service.)

Any amendment of this certificate, or erasure, or failure to complete any part of it, may render it invalid.

LA VALIDITÉ DE CE CERTIFICAT couvre une période de six mois commençant six jours après la première injection du vaccin ou, dans le cas d'une revaccination au cours de cette période de six mois, le jour de cette revaccination. (Aux États Unis deux injections sont données aux séries initiales.)

Le cachet d'authentification doit être conforme au modèle prescrit par l'administration sanitaire du territoire où la vaccination est effectuée. (Aux États Unis ce cachet doit être celui du Service d'Hygiène, de l'état, de la ville ou du comté où le vaccinateur exerce la médecine, du Département de la Défense, d'un centre désigné de vaccination contre la fièvre jaune, le sceau du Service de la Santé Publique des États Unis, ou le timbre spécial "S–C" approuvé par ce service.)

Toute correction ou rature sur le certificat ou l'omission d'une quelconque des mentions qu'il comporte peut affecter sa validité.

vaccination certificate requirements

"Under the International Sanitary Regulations a health authority may, under certain conditions, require certificates of vaccination against cholera, small-pox and yellow fever from travellers.

"Travellers should be advised that the requirements of countries of arrival are related not only to the health conditions prevailing in the country of departure but also to conditions in countries in which the traveller disembarks during the journey, except if he travels on a non-infected aircraft and (a) remains in the direct transit area of an airport; or (b) submits to the measures of segregation prescribed by the health authority, if the airport is not provided with a direct transit area; or (c) disembarks solely in order to continue his voyage from another airport in the vicinity, the transfer being made under the control of the health authority.

"The international certificates of vaccination are *individual* certificates. They should not be used collectively. Separate certificates should be issued for children; the information should not be incorporated in the mother's certificate."

Excerpts from Page 3, *Vaccination Certificate Requirements for International Travel—Situation as of 1 January 1968*. Published by the International Quarantine Service, World Health Organization, 1211 Geneva, Switzerland. 1968.

YELLOW-FEVER ENDEMIC ZONE IN AMERICA

This zone is bounded by a line beginning on the Pacific coast of Colombia at the 5° North parallel of latitude and extending east along that parallel of latitude to the eastern slopes of the Central Cordillera to an elevation of 2000 metres; thence southwards along the eastern slopes to the Central Cordillera and the Andes Mountains, at the same elevation to the boundary of Bolivia and Argentina; thence eastwards and northwards along the southern and eastern boundaries of Bolivia to the 15° South parallel of latitude; thence eastwards along that parallel of latitude to the western boundary of the State of Goiás; thence northwards along that boundary and the western boundary of the State of Maranhão to the Atlantic coast; thence along the Atlantic and Caribbean coasts of America to the eastern boundary of Costa Rica; thence along that boundary to the Pacific coast and thence along the Pacific coast of Panama and Colombia to the 5° North parallel of latitude. In addition, the Ilhéus and Itabuna Districts in the State of Bahía in Brazil bounded on the north by the River Contas, on the west by the 40° West meridian of longitude, on the south by the River Pardo and on the east by the Atlantic Ocean are included in the yellow-fever endemic zone. The ports and cities of Manaos in Brazil, Barranquilla, Cartagena and Bogotá in Colombia, together with the ports of the Republic of Panama and the Canal Zone, are excluded from the yellow-fever endemic zone. The continued exclusion of these ports and cities is, however, contingent on their maintenance of an *Aedes aegypti* index not exceeding 1%* as reported quarterly to WHO.

---

* Should at any time the index exceed 1% in any of the localities excluded from the endemic zone, information to that effect must immediately be notified to WHO.

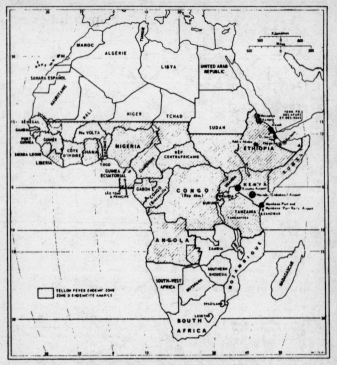

YELLOW-FEVER ENDEMIC ZONE IN AFRICA

The delineation is as follows: from the mouth of the River Senegal along that river eastwards to the 15° North parallel of latitude; thence eastwards along that parallel to the western border of the Sudan; thence southwards along that border to the 12° North parallel; thence eastwards along that parallel to the eastern border of the Sudan; thence northwards along that border to the Red Sea coast; thence southwards along the eastern coast of Africa to the northern boundary of the French Territory of the Afars and the Issas; thence along that boundary successively westwards, southwards and eastwards to the southern boundary of Somalia (Northern Region) and along that boundary eastwards and northwards to the eastern coast of Africa and thence along this coast to the southern boundary of Tanzania (Tanganyika); thence westwards along that boundary to its junction with the eastern boundary of the Congo (Democratic Rep.); thence westwards and southwards along the boundary of the Congo (Democratic Rep.) to the 10° South parallel of latitude; thence westwards along that parallel to the eastern border of Angola; thence southwards along that border and then along the eastern boundary of Balovale District** and Barotse Province** (Zambia) to the northern border of South-West Africa; thence westwards along that border to the west coast of Africa; thence northwards along the west coast of Africa to the mouth of the River Senegal, including the islands of the Gulf of Guinea. Excluded from the endemic zone are: the French Territory of the Afars and the Issas and the Northern Region of Somalia; Assab, Massawa, an area of 10 kilometers in radius from the centre of Asmara and an area of 20 kilometres in radius from the centre of Addis Ababa (Ethiopia); Kisumu airport, Nairobi airport, Mombasa port and Mombasa airport (Kenya). The continued exclusion of these areas is, however, contingent on their maintenance of an *Aedes aegypti* index not exceeding 1%* in Assab and Massawa, in and around Asmara, in Jibuti, Berbera and Hargeisa, in the airports of Kisumu and Nairobi and in the port and airport of Mombasa, as reported quarterly to WHO.

* Should, at any time, the index exceed 1% in any of the localities excluded from the endemic zone, information to that effect must immediately be notified to WHO.

check list—
going over

- Check-up by family physician at least one month before departure.
- Necessary records: X-ray reports, EKG, Lab tests, special precautions, etc.
- **Immunizations**
International Regulations Requirement
> Smallpox
> Yellow Fever
> Cholera

Always Recommended
> Tetanus/Diphtheria
> Polio
> Typhoid

Sometimes Recommended
> Typhus
> Plague
> Influenza
> Tuberculosis
> Rabies
> Hepatitis (Gamma globulin)

Children: All recommendations above plus
> Pertussis
> Measles

- **Medical Kit**

  For all:
  - Motion sickness pills
  - Antiseptics
  - Fever thermometer
  - First aid kit
  - Aspirin
  - Antidiarrheal medicine
  - Antifungus powder and ointment
  - Water purification tablets
  - Hygiene products
  - Toilet articles

- **Special Medications**
  - Sedatives
  - Tranquillizers
  - Other

- **Check Clothing for Climate and Area**

check list—
over there

Know how to find a doctor in the countries to be visited.

Water
    Boil it
    Use purification tablets or iodine drops
    Use bottled water

Food
    Avoid salads, raw vegetables, sauces,
    milk products

Colds
    Nose drops
    Aspirin
    Antihistamines

Allergies
    Antihistamines

Insomnia
    Sedative

Constipation
    Figs
    Bran cereal
    Milk of Magnesia tablets

Feet
Foot powder
Corn plasters

Back
Bed board

Dental
Dental floss
Oil of cloves

General Hygiene
Soap, toilet tissue, sanitary pads, facial tissue packets

First Aid Kit
Band aids
Antiseptic
Gauze
Tape
Scissors

Miscellaneous
Extra pair of eyeglasses plus prescription
Denture cleanser
Medic alert tags for specific diseases: Diabetes Epilepsy, etc.

area-by-area check list

Pages to check especially if you are going to . . .

U. S. Posts and Missions Abroad
addresses and telephone numbers

Abidjan, Ivory Coast (E)
 (Boite Postale 1712)
 Rue Crosson Duplessis et
  Boulevard Pelieu
 Tel: 260-31/34
Accra, Ghana (E)
 (P.O. Box 194)
 Liberia and Rowe Rds.
 Tel: 66811
Adana, Turkey (C)
 Ataturk Caddesi
 Tel: 3555
Addis Ababa, Ethiopia (E)
 Tel: 10666
 Crown Prince Asfaw Wossen St.
Adelaide, South Australia,
 Australia (C)(SP)
 The M.L.C. Bldg., Victoria Sq.
 Tel: 51-2664
Aden, Southern Yemen (E)
 Steamer Pt. (Tawahi)
 Tel: 2881, 2882
Aleppo, Syrian Arab Republic (CG)
 Sebil Quarter
 Tel: 17600, 17601
Alexandria, United Arab
 Republic (CG)
 2 Ave. El Horreya
 Tel: 22861, 25607, 38941
Algiers, Algeria (E)
 Villa Mektoub, Chemin Beaure-
  paire, Colonne Voiro
 Tel: 60-14-25 through 29,
  60-36-70 through 72
Amman, Jordan (E)
 Jabel Luwaibdeh
 Tel: 22387-8-9
Amsterdam, Netherlands (CG)
 Museumplein No. 19
 Tel: 790321, 790442, 791052

Ankara, Turkey (E)

110 Ataturk Blvd.
 Tel: 125050
Antwerp, Belgium (CG)
 101 Frankrijklei
 Tel: 32-18-00
Arequipa, Peru (CA)
 San Juan de Dios 112
 Tel: 6687
Asmara, Ethiopia (CG)
 32 Franklin D. Roosevelt St.
 Tel: 10855
Asuncion, Paraguay (E)
 1776 Mariscal Lopez Ave.
 Tel: 4301-07
Athens, Greece (E)
 91 Queen Sophia Ave.
 Tel: 712951, 718401
Auckland, New Zealand (C)
 Queen St. and Victoria St., East
 Tel: 32-526
Baghdad, Iraq (E)
 Mansur St.
 Tel: 34171
Baida, Libya (Office)
 (no street address)
Bamako, Mali (E)
 Rue Testard and Rue Mohamed V
 Tel: 22.92
Bangkok, Thailand (E)
 95 Wireless Rd.
 Tel: 59800-14
Bangui, Central African
 Republic (E)
 Sq. de la Republique Centra-
  fricaine
 Tel: 2050, 2051
Barcelona, Spain (CG)
 Via Layetana 33
 Tel: 222.2044
Barranquilla, Colombia (C)
 34th St., No. 43-31

Tel: 11.650

Basra, Iraq (C)
Sharia Hurriyah
Tel: 4231-2-3

Bathurst, The Gambia (E)
(P.O. Box 596) 8 Cameron Street
Tel: 526

Beirut, Lebanon (E)
Corniche at Rue Aiv Mreisseh
Tel: 240800

Belém, Pará, Brazil (C)
Avenida Oswaldo Cruz 165
Tel: 4557

Belfast, Northern Ireland (CG).
See United Kingdom.
Queen's House, 14 Queen St. (1)
Tel: 28239

Belgrade, Yugoslavia (E)
Kneza Milosa 50
Tel: 645655

Belize City, British Honduras (C)
See United Kingdom.
Gabourel Lane and Hutson St.
Tel: 221

Belo Horizonte, Minas Gerais,
Brazil (C)(SP)
Rua Goitacazes, 14, 12th floor
Tel: 4-9339, 4-9321

Benghazi, Libya (Office)
Sharia El Slawi
Tel: 3027-8-9, 2050

Berlin, Germany (M)
170 Clayallee
Tel: 76 43 15

Bern, Switzerland (E)
93/95 Jubilaumsstrasse
Tel: 43 00 11

Bilbao, Spain (C)
Plaza de los Alfereces Pro-
visionales, 2-4°
Tel: 217966, 217967

Blantyre, Malawi
(P.O. Box 380)
Nyrho House, Victoria Ave.
Tel: 438

Bogotá, Colombia (E)
Edificio Bavaria

Carrera 10, No. 28-49
Tel: 349-560

Bombay, India (CG)
"Lincoln House", 78 Bhulabhai
Desai Rd.
Tel: 77441 through 77448

Bonn, Germany (E)
Mehlemer Ave., Bad Godesberg
Tel: 1955 Bad Godesberg

Bordeaux, France (CG)
No. 4 rue Esprit-des-Lois
Tel: 52. 65. 95

Brasilia, Brazil (Office)
Avenida das Nacoes, Lote No. 3
Tel: 5-5422

Brazzaville, Republic of Congo (E)
Ave. du 28 Aout 1940
Tel: 31.06

Bremen, Germany (CG)
Prasident-Kennedy-Platz
Tel: 32-00-01

Bridgetown, Barbados (E)
Canadian Imperial
Bank of Commerce Bldg,
4th fl, Broad St.
Tel: 3574/75/76/77

Brisbane, Queensland, Australia (C)
359 Queen St.
Tel: 31-2649

Brussels, Belgium (E)
27 Blvd. du Regent
Tel: 13. 38. 30

Brussels, Belgium
(USNATO). See
U. S. Mission to the North
Atlantic Treaty Organization
Tel: 41-00-40

Bucharest, Romania (E)
Strada Tudor Argezhi No. 9
Tel: 12-40-40

Budapest, Hungary (E)
V, Szabadsag Ter 12
Tel: 329-375
(after office hours: 119-629)

Buenaventura, Colombia (CA)

Buenos Aires, Argentina (E)

Sarmiento Bldg. 663
Tel: 3475–91
Bujumbura, Burundi (E)
(Boite Postale 1720)
Chaussee d'Astrida
Tel: 31-34
Bukavu, Democratic Republic of
the Congo (C)
(Boite Postale 1697)
4th Ave. Leopold I
Tel: 3064-3074
Cairo, United Arab Republic (E)
5, Sharia al Zekra
Tel: 28219
Calcutta, India (CG)
5/1 Harrington Street
Tel: 44-3611 through 44-3616
Calgary, Alberta, Canada (CG)
805 Eighth Ave., S.W.
Tel: 266-8962
Cali, Colombia (C)
Edificio Pielroja (Carrera 3,
#11-55)
Tel: 88136, 88137
Canada
Canary Islands. See Spain.
Canberra, Australian Capital Ter-
ritory, Australia (E)
Moonah Pl., Yarralumla, A.C.T.
Tel: 7-1351
Cape Town, Cape Province,
Republic of South Africa (CG)
Heerengracht, Foreshore
Tel: 3-7061
Caracas, Venezuela (E)
Avenida Francisco de Miranda
and Avenida Principal de la
Floresta
Tel: 33-86-61
Casablanca, Morocco (CG)
1 Place de la Fraternite
Tel: 60521/22/23; 60562
Cebu, Philippines (C)
Philippine American Life In-
surance Bldg., Jones Ave.
Tel: 4661, 4662

Chiang Mai, Thailand (C)

Vichayanond Rd.
Tel: 203
Chihuahua,
Chihuahua, Mexico (C)(SP)
Ciudad Juárez, Chihuahua,
Mexico (C)
1896 Ave. 16 de Septiembre
Tel: 22510
Cochabamba, Bolivia (C)
Calle Espana 345
Tel: 4780, 4781
Colombo, Ceylon (E)
44 Galle Rd., Colpetty
6216 through 6219
Conakry, Guinea (E)
(Boite Postale 603)
Tel: 2478, 2494, and 2160
Constantine, Algeria (C)
Rue J. F. Kennedy
Tel: 73.86, 73.87
Copenhagen, Denmark (E)
Dag Hammarskjolds Alle 24
Tel: TRia 4505
Cotonou, Dahomey (E)
Rue Caporal Anani Bernard
Tel: 26-93
Curacao, Netherlands Antilles (CG)
St. Anna Blvd. 19, vice
John B. Gorsiraweg No. 1
Tel: 13306
Czechoslovakia, [Czechoslovak
Socialist Republic]
Dacca, Pakistan (CG)
Adamjee Court Bldg., Montijheel
Area
Tel: 44241 through 44245
Dakar, Senegal (E)
(Boite Postale 49)
BAO Bldg., Place de
l'Independence
Tel: 26344/45;22143
Damascus, Syrian Arab Republic (E)
Chare (Avenue) al-Mansour,
Abu Rummanih
Tel: 32555-6-7

Dar es Salaam, Tanzania (E)
National Bank of Commerce Bldg.

(City Drive Br) on City Dr,
P.O. Box 9123
Tel: 22775
David, Panama (C)
c/o American Embassy, Panama
Dhahran, Saudi Arabia (CG)
(no street address)
Djakarta, Indonesia (E)
Medan Merdeka, Selatan 5
Tel: 40001-9
Douala, Cameroon (C)
Blvd du General LeClerc, B.P.4006
Tel: 32-31, 40-93
Dublin, Ireland (E)
42 Elgin Rd., Ballsbridge
Tel: 64061/9
Durban, Natal, Republic of South
Africa (CG)
1400 Norwich Union House
6 Durban Club Place
Tel: 28388, 28389, 28380
Düsseldorf, Germany (CG)
5 Cecilien Allee
Tel: 490081
Edinburgh, Scotland (CG). See
United Kingdom.
3 Regent Ter.
Tel: 031-556 8315
Enugu, Nigeria (C)
1 A Ogui Road
Tel: 3318
Florence, Italy (C)
38 Lungarno Amerigo Vespucci
Tel: 298-276
Fort-Lamy, Chad (E)
Rue du Lt. Col. Colonna
d'Ornano
Tel: 28-40
Frankfurt am Main, Germany (CG)
6 Frankfurt am Main, 21
Siesmayerstrasse
Tel: 770731
Freetown, Sierra Leone (E)
Walpole/Westmoreland Streets
Tel: 6481
Fukuoka, Japan (C)
5-26 Ohori 2-chome

Tel: 75-9331/4
Gaberones, Botswana (E)
Barclays Bank Bldg.
P.O. Box 90
Geneva, Switzerland (European
Office of United Nations and
Other International Organiza-
tions). See U.S. Missions to
International Organizations.
Genoa, Italy (CG)
Banca d'America e d'Italia Bldg
Piazza Portello 6
Tel: 282-741 to 282-745
Georgetown, Guyana (E)
31 Main St.
Tel: 2686
Göteborg, Sweden (CG)
Vasagatan 43 B
Tel: 18-70-00
Great Britain, and Northern
Ireland, [United Kingdom of]
See United Kingdom.
Guadalajara, Jalisco, Mexico (CG)
489 16th of September
Tel: 3-29-95 through 98
Guatemala, Guatemala (E)
8a. Avenida 11-65
Tel: 23201 through 23209
Guayaquil, Ecuador (CG)
9 de Octobre and Garcia Moreno
Tel: 11-570
Hague, The, Netherlands (E)
102 Lange Voorhout
Tel: 62-49-11
Halifax, Nova Scotia, Canada (CG)
Bank of Nova Scotia Bldg.
Hollis St. and Prince St
Tel: 423-9387, 423-9388
Hamburg, Germany (CG)
Alsterufer 27/28
Tel: 44-10-61
Hamilton, Bermuda (CG). See
United Kingdom.
Vallis Bldg., Front St.
Tel: 1-2908, 1-2909
Hargeisa, Somali Republic Office (SP)
Helsinki, Finland (E)

Itainen Kaivopuisto 21
Tel: 11931
Hermosillo, Mexico (CG)
Issteson Bldg, 3d fl., Blvd.
Centenario
y Miguel Hidalgo y Costilla
Tel: 3-89-23/5
Hong Kong (CG). *See United Kingdom.*
26 Garden Rd.
Tel: 23-9011
Ibadan, Nigeria (C)
Western Region Finance Corp.
Lebanon St.
Tel: 24101, 24102
Isfahan, Iran (C)
Ave. Chahar Bagh
Tel: 3580
Istanbul, Turkey (CG)
147 Mesrutiyet Caddesi
Tel: 444880
Izmir, Turkey (CG)
65/3 Cumhuriyet Bulvari
Tel: 32136
Jerusalem (CG)
(2 offices)
Agron Rd.
via Israel
Tel: 2-4491
Nablus Rd.
via Israel
Tel: 82231
Jidda, Saudi Arabia (E)
Palestine Rd., Ruwais
Tel: 2101-2-3
Johannesburg, Transvaal, Repub-
lic of South Africa (CG)
521 So. African Mutual Bldg.
Tel: 834-3051
Kabul, Afghanistan (E)
Ansari Wat, Karte-E Wali
Tel: 24230-9
Kaduna, Nigeria (C)
5 Ahmadu Bello Way
Tel: 3373-76, 2134
Kampala, Uganda (E)
(P.O. Box 7007)

Embassy House, 9-11 Obote
Ave.
Tel: 54451
Karachi, Pakistan (Office)
Victoria Rd. and Frere Garden
Tel: 55081
Kathmandu, Nepal (E)
King's Way
Tel: 11199
Khartoum, Sudan (E)
(P.O. Box 699)
Gamhouria Ave.
Tel: 71155-59
Khorramshahr, Iran (C)
Pahlavi St.
Tel: 3612
Kigali, Rwanda (E)
13 Blvd. Central
Tel: 191
Kingston, Jamaica (E)
No. 43 Duke St.
Tel: 26341
Kinshasa, Democratic Republic
of the Congo (E)
6 Ave. des Aviateurs
Tel: 5881, 5882
Kisangani, Democratic Republic
of the Congo (C)
(Boite Postale 515)
Ave. Eisenhower
Tel: 2957, 2958
Kobe, Japan (CG). *See*
Osaka-Kobe.
Kuala Lumpur, Malaysia (E)
A.I.A. Bldg.,
Jalan Ampang
Tel: 26321
Kuching, Malaysia (C)(SP)
c/o American Embassy,
Kuala Lumpur
Kuwait, Kuwait (E)
(no street address)
Tel: 39254, 39260, 39388
Lagos, Nigeria, (E)
1 King's College Rd.
Tel: 22741

La Paz, Bolivia (E)
Banco Popular del Peru Bldg.,
corner of Calles Mercado y
Colon
Tel: 6370

Las Palmas, Gran Canaria,
See Spain. Canary Islands (CA)

Letyia, 32

Libreville, Gabon (E)
"Mora Residence"
Tel: 003, 004

Liechtenstein, [Principality of]

Lima, Peru (E)
Avenidas Wilson and Espana
Tel: 30660

Lisbon, Portugal (E)
Avenida Duque de Loule No. 39
Tel: 555140 through 555149

Liverpool, England (CG). See
United Kingdom.
Cunard Bldg., Pierhead
Central 8501

Lomé, Togo (E)
Rue Pelletier and rue Victor
Hugo
Tel: 29-91

London, England (E). See United
Kingdom.
24/31 Grosvenor Sq., W. 1
GRosvenor 9000

Lourenco Marques, Mozambique,
Africa (CG). See Portugal.
No. 3 Rua Salazar
Tel: 6051, 6052

Luanda, Angola, Africa (CG). See
Portugal.
Avenida Paulo Dias de Novais,
37
Tel: 7591, 70155

Lubumbashi, Democratic Republic
of the Congo (C)
(Boite Postale 1196)
1029 Blvd. Elisabeth
Tel: 2324, 2325

Lusaka, Zambia (E)
(P.O. Box 1617)

David Livingstone Rd. &
Independence Ave.
Tel: 50222

Luxembourg, Luxembourg (E)
22 Blvd. Emmanuel Servais
Tel: 40123-4-5-6-7

Lyon, France (CG)
7 Quai Général Sarrail
Tel: 24-68-49

Madras, India (CG)
150-B Mount Rd.
Tel: 83041

Madrid, Spain (E)
Serrano, 75
Tel: 276-3400

Malé, Maldive Islands (E)
(No office maintained)

Malta

Managua, Nicaragua (E)
Blvd. Somoza
Tel: 6771

Manaus, Amazonas, Brazil (CA)

Mandalay, Burma (C)(SP)
71st St. & South Moat Rd.
Tel: 555

Manila, Philippines (E)
1201 Roxas Blvd.
Tel: 5-80-11

Maracaibo, Venezuela (C)
Edificio Matema Avenida 15
Calle 78
Tel: 71171, 71172

Marseille, France (CG)
No. 9 Rue Armeny
Tel: 33-78-33 through 33-78-37

Martinique, French West Indies (C)
See France.
10 Rue Schoelcher, Fort-de-
France
Tel: 30.01

Maseru, Lesotho (E)
P.O. Box 333
Tel: 266

Matamores, Tamaulipas, Mexico (C)(SP)
First St.
Tel: 2-0241, 2-1241

Mauritius

Mazatlan, Sinaloa, Mexico (C)
Avenida del Mar
Tel: 28-85, 26-87

Mbabane, Kingdom of Swaziland (E)
Tel: (Not available)

Medan, Indonesia (C)
13 Djalan Imam Bondjol
Tel: 22290

Medellin, Colombia (C)
Edificio Santa Helena
Avenida Primero de Mayo
Tel: 313-188

Melbourne, Victoria, Australia (CG)
14-22 Commercial Rd.
Tel: 26-1651

Merida, Yucatan, Mexico (C)
Calle 56A No. 453
Tel: 60-30, 26-03

Mexicali, Baja California, Mexico
(C)
Avenida Arista 1974
Tel: 762-6303/6312/6313

Mexico, D. F., Mexico (E)
Cor. Danubio and Paseo de la
Reforma
305, Colonia Cuauhtemoc
Tel: 25-91-00

Milan, Italy (CG)
Piazza della Republica 32
Tel: 652841-2-3-4-5

Mogadiscio, Somali Republic (E)
Corso Primo Luglio
Tel: 216, 259, 288, 289

Monaco, Monaco (C)
(Office maintained at Nice,
France)

Monrovia, Liberia (E)
United Nations Dr.
Tel: 22991, 22992

Monterrey, Nuevo León, Mexico
(CG)
Avenida Juarez 800 Sur
Tel: 3 06 50

Montevideo, Uruguay (E)
Avenida Agracida 1458

Tel: 8-97-45 through 49

Montreal, Quebec, Canada (CG)
1558 McGregor Ave.
Tel: WELLington 7-6301

Montreal, Quebec, Canada (ICAO).
See U.S. Missions to International Organizations.

Morelia, Michoacán, Mexico (C)(SP)
APDO Postal 135
Tel: 2-26-24

Moscow, Union of Soviet Socialist
Republics (E)
Ulitsa Chaykovskogo 19/21/23
Tel: 252-00-11 through 252-00-19

Munich, Germany (CG)
5 Koeniginstrasse
Tel: 23-0-11

Muscat, The Sultanate of Muscat
and Oman (C)
(Office maintained at Aden)

Nagoya, Japan (C)
9-3, Sannomaru 1-chrome,
Naku-ku
Tel: 231-7791 through 7795

Naha, Okinawa (Consular Unit).
See Japan.
Bldg. 405, Hawaii Circle, Army
Wheel Base, Naha Area
Tel: 72981

Nairobi, Kenya (E)
(P.O. Box 30137)
Cotts House on Eliot St.
Tel: 20381

Naples, Italy (CG)
Piazza Principe di Napoli
Tel: 380440-1-2-3-4

Nassau, New Providence,
Bahamas (CG). *See* United
Kingdom.
Adderly Bldg.
Tel: 2-1181 (23040 after hours
and weekends)

New Delhi, India (E)
Shanti Path, Chanakyapuri 21
Tel: 70351

Niamey, Niger (E)
  Boite Postale 201
  Tel: 26-63,26-64

Nice, France (C)
  No. 3 Rue Dr. Barety
  Tel: 88-89-55, 88-89-56, 88-72-65

Nicosia, Cyprus (E)
  Therissos St. and Dositheos St.
  Tel: 5151

Nogales, Sonora, Mexico (C)(SP)
  Ave. Obregon 31 Altos
  P.O. Box 1090, Nogales,
  Arizona, 85621
  Tel: 596, 305

North Atlantic Treaty Organization
  (NATO), International Staff,
  Brussels, Belgium. *See* U. S.
  Missions to International
  Organizations

Northern Ireland, [United Kingdom
  of] Great Britain and
  See United Kingdom.

Nouakchott, Mauritania (E)
  American Embassy, BP 222
  Tel: 20-60

Nuevo Laredo, Tamaulipas,
  Mexico (C)
  Calle Madero and Avenida
  Ocampo
  Tel: 2-00-05

Oporto, Portugal (C)
  Apartado #88
  Rua Julio Dinis, 826-3°
  Tel: 6-3094/95/96

Oran, Algeria (C)
  25 rue Lamaratime
  (unavailable)

Osaka-Kobe, Japan (CG)
  10 Kano-cho 6-chrome, Ikuta
  Ku (Kobe)
  Tel: 33-6865/9

Oslo, Norway (E)
  Drammensveien 18
  Tel: 56-68-80

Ottawa, Ontario, Canada (E)
  100 Wellington St

Tel: CEntral 6-2341

Ouagadougou, Upper Volta (E)
  Boite Postale 35
  Tel: 21-91, 21-92

Palermo, Italy (CG)
  Via Marchese di Villabianca
  Angolo Via Vaccarini
  Tel: 215534-5-6-7

Palma de Mallorca, Spain (CA)

Panama, Panama (E)
  Avenida Balboa at 38th St.
  Tel: Panama 5-3600 Balboa
  (Zone) 2-1248

Paramaribo, Surinam (CG). *See*
  Netherlands.
  Kerkplein 1
  Tel: 3024

Paris, France (E)
  2 Ave. Gabriel
  Tel: ANjou 7460

Paris, France (USOECD). *See*
  U.S. Missions to International
  Organizations.

Perth, Western Austrailia, Australia (C)
  171 St. George's Ter.
  Tel: 21-5929

Peshawar, Pakistan (C)
  New Municipal Bldg.
  Tel: 2003, 2004

Piedras Negras, Coahuila, Mexico
  (C)(SP)
  P.O. Box AA, Eagle Pass, Tex.,
  78852
  Avenida Emilio Carranzo No.
  1103
  Tel: 34

Piura, Peru (CA)

Ponta Delgada, Sao Miguel, Azores
  (C). *See* Portugal.
  Avenida D. Henrique
  Tel: 22216, 22217

Port-au-Prince, Haiti (E)
  Harry Truman Blvd.
  Tel: 2665, 3533

Port Louis, Mauritius (E)

Port Said, United Arab Republic
(C)
Sultan Hussein St.
Tel: 4705, 8000

Porto Alegre, Rio Grande do Sul,
Brazil (C)
Rua Uruguai, 155, 11th floor
Tel: 8516, 5657

Port-of-Spain, Trinidad and Tobago
(E)
15 Queen's Park West
Tel: 21171

Poznan, Poland (C)
Ulica Chopina 4
Tel: 95-86, 91-62

Prague, Czechoslovakia (E)
Trziste 15
Tel: 531-456 through 459

Pretoria, Transvaal, Republic of
South Africa (E)
Navarre Trust Bldg.,
Pretorius St.
Tel: 33031-9

Puerto la Cruz, Anzoátegui,
Venezuela (C)
Carretara Negra
Tel: 1170

Puntarenas, Costa Rica (GA)

Quebec, Quebec, Canada (CG)
No. 1 Ave. Ste-Genevieve
Tel: 522-7089

Quito, Ecuador (E)
120 Avenida Patria
Tel: 30020

Rabat, Morocco (E)
6 Avenue de Marrakech
Tel: 30361/62/63/64/65

Rangoon, Burma (E)
581 Merchant St.
Tel: 18055

Rawalpindi, Pakistan (E)
57-A Satellite Town
Tel: 64975-64977

Recife, Pernambuco, Brazil (CG)
Rua Goncalves Maia 163
Tel: 2-6612, 2-6577, 4-1599

Reykjavik, Iceland (E)

Laufasvegur 21
Tel: 24083

Riga, Latvia

Rio de Janeiro, Brazil (E)
147 Avenida Presidente Wilson
Tel: 52-8055

Rome, Italy (E)
Via V. Veneto 119
Tel: 4674

Rome, Italy (FAO). See U.S. Mission
to International Organizations.

Rotterdam, Netherlands (CG)
Vlasmarkt 1
Tel: 11. 75. 60

Saigon, Viet-Nam (E)
39 Ham Nghi Blvd.
Tel: 25251

Saint John, New Brunswick,
Canada (C)
Suite 701, Harbour Bldg.,
133 Prince William St.
Tel: 692-1519

St. John's, Newfoundland, Canada
(CG)
King's Bridge Rd.
Tel: 726-4524

Salisbury, Southern Rhodesia (CG).
See United Kingdom.
(P.O. Box 2895)
48 Gordon Ave.
Tel: 28066, 28067

Salvador, Brazil (C)(SP)
Edificio Serra da Raiz,
Rua Grécia 8, 7th floor
Tel: 2-1405 and 2-1406

San José, Costa Rica (E)
Avenido 3 and Calle 1
Tel: (unavailable)

San Luis Potosi, Mexico (C)(SP)
Apartado Postal 697
Tel: (Unavailable)

San Marino, San Marino (C)
(Office maintained at Florence
Italy)

San Pedro Sula, Honduras (C)
Blvd. de Circunvalacion
Tel: 10-82, 15-91

San Salvador, El Salvador (E)
No. 1230, 25 Avenida Norte
Tel: 25-7100

San'a, Yemen (E)
(unavailable)
Tel: (unavailable)

Santa Isabel, Equatorial Guinea (E)

Santiago, Chile (E)
1343 Augustinas
Tel: 82801-4

Santiago de los Caballeros,
Dominican Republic (C)
(unavailable)
Tel: (unavailable)

Santo Domingo, Dominican
Republic (E)
Calle Cesar Nicolas Pensen and
Calle Leopoldo Navarro
Tel: 54141

Sao Luis, Maranhao, Brazil (CA)

Sao Miguel, Azores.

Sao Paulo, Sao Paulo, Brazil (CG)
Edificio Conjunto Nacional,
Rua Padre João Manuel, 20
Tel: 37-5574

Sapporo, Japan (C)
North 1 West 13
Tel: 22-5121/3

Scarborough, Trinidad and
Tobago (CA)

Seoul, Korea (E)
82 Sejong-Ro
Tel: 72-2601 thru 2619

Seville, Spain (CG)
Paseo de Las Delicias No. 7
Tel: 31996

Singapore, Singapore (E)
No. 30 Hill St.
Tel: 30251

Sofia, Bulgaria (E)
1 Alexander Stamboliski Blvd.
Tel: 88-48-01/88-48-05

Stockholm, Sweden (E)
Strandvägen 101
Tel: 63.05.20

Strasbourg, France (CG)
15 Ave. d'Alsace
Tel: 35.31.04-5-6

Stuttgart, Germany (CG)
7 Urbanstrasse
Tel: 246 341

Surabaya, Indonesia (C)
Djalan Raya Dr. Sutomo 33
Tel: Selatan 836 and 837
Darmo 7545

Suva, Fifi Islands (C). *See* United
Kingdom.
Jogia-Mistry Bldg., Cumming St.
Tel: 5304, 5305

Sydney, New South Wales,
Australia (CG)
George and Wynyard Sts.
Tel: 29-2101

Tabriz, Iran (C)
Shahnaz Ave.
Tel: 2101, 5487

Taipei, Taiwan (E). *See* China
1842 Chung Cheng Rd.
Tel: 33551-6

Taiz, Yemen (Office)
Main St.
Tel: (unavailable)

Tampico, Tamaulipas, Mexico (C)
Diaz Miron 106 Oriente
Tel: 2-21-89, 2-20-89

Tananarive, Malagasy Republic (E)
(Boite Postale 620)
14 rue Rainitovo, Antsahavola
Tel: 42-57, 42-59

Tangier, Morocco (CG)
Chemin des Amoureaux
Tel: 15904/05/06; 15571/72/73

Tegucigalpa, Honduras (E)
Avenida La Paz
Tel: 2-3121 through 2-3124;
2-3127

Tehran, Iran (E)
Ave. Takti Jamshid and
Roosevelt Ave.
Tel: 60511, 60711

Tel Aviv, Israel (E)

71 Hayarkon St.
Tel: 56171

Thessaloniki, Greece (CG)
59 King Konstantine St.
Tel: 73-941

Tijuana, Baja California, Mexico
(CG)
Blvd. Agua Caliente 470
Tel: Du 5-22-85

Togo, [Republic of]

Tokyo, Japan (E)
2 of No. 1 Enokizaka-cho
Tel: 481-7141

Toronto, Ontario, Canada (CG)
360 University Ave.
Tel: EMpire 6-3553

Trieste, Italy (C)
Via Galatti 1
Tel: 30221

Tripoli, Libya (E)
Via Grazioli
Tel: 42500, 45385

Tunis, Tunisia (E)
186 Ave. de Paris
Tel: 282. 518

Turin, Italy (C)
Via Alfieri 17
Tel: 43600, 43610, 513-367

Udorn, Thailand (C)(SP)
Photic Rd. Udorn Dhani

U.S. Mission to the European Com-
munities (USEC), Brussels and
Luxembourg
23, Ave. Des Arts, Brussels,
Belgium
Tel: 13.44.50
35 Blvd. Royal, Luxembourg,
Luxembourg
Tel: 24353

U.S. Mission to the European
Office of United Nations and
Other Internation Organizations, Geneva. See U.S.
Missions to International Organizations.
80 Rue du Lausanne, Geneva,

Switzerland
Tel: 31-80-00

U.S. Mission to the International
Atomic Energy Agency (IAEA),
Vienna. See U.S. Missions to
International Organizations.
14 Schmidgasse, Vienna, Austria
Tel: 34-75-11

U.S. Mission to the International
Civil Aviation Organization
(ICAO), Montreal. See U.S.
Missions to International Orga-
nizations.
901 International Aviation
Bldg., Montreal, Quebec,
Canada
Tel: University 6-5028

U.S. Mission to the North
Atlantic Treaty Organization
(USNATO), Brussels. See
U.S. Missions to International
Organizations.
27 Boulevard du Regent
Brussels 1, Belgium
Tel: 41-00-40

U.S. Mission to the Organization for
Economic Cooperation and Develop-
ment (USOECD), Paris. See U.S.
Missions to International Organiza-
tions.
2 rue de la Faisanderi,
Paris, France
Tel: ANjou 6440

Vaduz, Liechtenstein (CG)
(Office maintained at Zurich,
Switzerland)

Valencia, Spain (C)
No. 74, Calle Colon
Tel: 21-11-08, 21-75-90,
22-54-96

Valletta, Malta (E)
Airways House,
Sliema, Malta
Tel: 36411

Valparaiso, Chile (CA)

Vancouver, British Columbia,
Canada (CG)

1030 W. Georgia St.
Tel: Mutual 5-4311

Veracruz, Veracruz, Mexico (C)
Arista ya Malecon
Tel: 2-30-40

Vienna, Austria (E)
Embassy Bldg. X, Boltzmann-
gasse 16
Tel: 346611, 347511

Vienna, Austria (IAEA). See U.S.
Missions to International Organizations

Vientiane, Laos (E)
Rue Bartholonie
Tel: 194

Warsaw, Poland (E)
Aleje Ujazdowskie 29/31
Tel: 283041-9

Wellington, New Zealand (E)
Government Life Insurance
Bldg., Customhouse Quay
Tel: 41-074

Windsor, Ontario, Canada (C)

500 Ouellette Ave.
Tel: 253-5203

Winnipeg, Manitoba, Canada
(CG)
6 Donald St.
Tel: 474-2394, 2395, 2396

Yaoundé, Cameroon (E)
(Boite Postale 817)
Rue Nachtigal
Tel: 33-57, 33-58

Yemen, Southern [People's
Republic of].
See Southern Yemen.

Zagreb, Yugoslavia (CG)
Zrinjevac 13
Tel: 440-811

Zanzibar, Tanzania (C)
83 A Tuzungumzeni Sq.,
Box No. 4
Tel: 2118, 2119

Zurich, Switzerland (CG)
Talacker 35
Tel: 23.07.10

index

THESE TWO BOOKS
COULD CHANGE YOUR LIFE

NEW HOPE FOR INCURABLE DISEASES

E. Cheraskin, M.D. and
W.M. Ringsdorf, Jr., M.D.

The revolutionary bestseller that proves in simple, everyday language that the battle against many dread diseases previously considered hopeless is being won—today. Stressing simple organic improvements in diet and nutrition and recent dramatic discoveries in these areas, the authors outline radically new and hopeful treatments for some of the most feared ailments of our time—multiple sclerosis, glaucoma, heart disease, mental retardation, birth defects and others. **"It is likely to become the most valuable guide to good health anyone could posess . . . an historic book, a must for all health seekers. The material on food supplements alone, is worth the price of the book." — Better Nutrition** $1.65

REVITALIZE YOUR BODY WITH NATURE'S SECRETS

Edwin Flatto, N.D., D.O.

A respected homeopathic physician explores every aspect of physical and mental well-being, never losing sight of the fact that health is the natural state of the body while disease is an unnatural state of imbalance. Fasting as a way to cleanse the body of toxic waste, the importance of a diet of wholesome, natural foods and the rewards of right eating are covered, as are exercise as therapy and the health benefits of fresh air and sunshine. Scores of questions on the problems of overweight, ulcers, varicose veins, acne, sinus trouble, constipation, colds and other common ailments are answered. Soundly scientific, easy-to-follow, this simple book promises lasting health, undreamed vigor and the happiness and peace that go with them.

$1.45

"THE MORE NATURAL OUR FOOD
THE BETTER OUR HEALTH"

SOYBEAN (PROTEIN) RECIPE IDEAS
Nancy Snider

As a major source of protein soybeans are a nutritious and endlessly versatile food. Here are over 100 unusual and delicious recipes that take the zesty soybean from breakfast to dinner in a fabulous cookbook by a noted home economist and food editor. Scores of diet and dollar stretching recipes—all easy to prepare and serve—and all featuring soy protein—soy stroganoff, meat loaf, soy breakfast items, soups, entrees, side dishes, sandwiches, breads, desserts, much more. Includes menu ideas and tips on cooking with soy.

Illustrated, 95¢

LOW-FAT COOKERY
Evelyn S. Stead and Gloria K. Warren

Here finally is the perfect cookbook for a calorie-conscious, health-happy age. Incorporating more than 250 delicious, easy-to-follow recipes, **Low-Fat Cookery** puts the fun into dietetic cooking—and even more imporant, dietetic eating. Imagine delicious low-fat recipes for baked lasagna, fruitcake, bleu-cheese dressing, butterscotch sauce and lobster newburg. Included are invaluable aids to dietetic cooking with an easy-to-remember summary of the basic points of low-fat cookery, how to modify any recipe to obtain a low-fat content, information about new food products to enrich and diversify a low-fat diet, and a helpful discussion of special diets such as restricted sodium and unsaturated vegetable oil plans. **$1.45**

NATURE'S OWN VEGETABLE COOKBOOK
Ann Williams-Heller

Over 350 mouthwatering vegetable recipes—complete with practical information on the buying, storing, cooking, seasoning and nutritional value of each vegetable. With this cookbook, noted nutritionist Ann Williams-Heller has opened the door to an entirely new culinary world. She brings her cooking genius to bear on every available vegetable—in main dishes, casseroles, salads, soups and their countless variations. Also included are recipes for sauces and salad dressings as well as nutrition charts that show the vitamin and mineral content of each vegetable. **$1.45**

Good Health Begins Right Here

ABC'S OF VITAMINS, MINERALS AND NATURAL FOODS

John Paul Latour

An accurate, up-to-the-minute guide to foods, vitamins, minerals and poisons—their use and abuse. Reveals what to eat and what **not** to eat to achieve radiant good health. **95¢**

ENCYCLOPEDIA OF MEDICINAL HERBS

Joseph Kadans, Ph.D.

A practical guide to the medical and cosmetic use of over 600 herbs—with hundreds of simple herbal treatments for all kinds of ailments. Special section on herb and spice cookery. **$1.45**

LITTLE-KNOWN SECRETS OF HEALTH AND LONG LIFE

Steve Prohaska

How to avoid doctors, dentists, hospitals and medical bills while gaining the blessings of good health and long life through simple, natural means. Features the fabulous Saturation Diet and a proven exercise program. **$5.95**

THE ARTHRITIS HANDBOOK

Darrell Crain, M.D.

An expert, authoritative guide to alleviating the suffering of arthritis, rheumatism and gout through natural diet and exercise. "A valuable manual."— The Arthritis Foundation **$1.45**

WINE AND BEER MAKING SIMPLIFIED

H.E. Bravery

The thinking man's handbook—a lucid and lively guide for the home winemaker who knows "what to do" but wants to know "why it works." With a section of recipes from apricot wine to light mild ale. **95¢**

HEALTH AND VIGOR AFTER 40 WITH NATURAL FOODS AND VITAMINS

Herman Saussele, D.C.

A practicing chiropractic doctor reveals how men and women in the middle years can start the powerful healing forces of nature working for better health, longer life and more joyful living. **$1.45**

HEALTH TONIC, ELIXIRS AND POTIONS FOR THE LOOK AND FEEL OF YOUTH

Carlson Wade

Scores of easy-to-make, easy-to-use tonics, potions, and elixirs said to bring relief from seemingly hopeless aches and pains and which may help you look and feel years younger than your actual age. **$1.45**

HEALTHIER JEWISH COOKERY
The Unsaturated Fat Way

June Roth

Hundreds of traditional Jewish recipes, streamlined to remove the saturated fats and retain the old-fashioned tastes. Substitutes vegetable for animal fat, eliminates frying, uses herbs and natural foods. **$4.95**

HEALTH and MEDICINE BOOKS